2 Palace of Westminster audio tour ➜ SB (p. 10)

03 Read a)–c) first. Then listen to the following audio guide to the Palace of Westminster and do the tasks.

a) Circle the right answers.

1 The section is about …

A the State Opening of Parliament. B the Government calendar. C the British Government.

2 The colour of the seats is …

A green. B red. C yellow.

3 It is held …

A in Buckingham Palace. B under the Houses of Parliament. C in the House of Lords chamber.

4 Who may take part?

A Lords, MPs and legal representatives B Lords and MPs only C Lords only

b) Match the shapes to the parliaments.

Althing in Iceland

House of Commons in UK

Bundestag in Germany

c) Answer the questions in notes.

1 Who has the highest position in the House of Commons? ______

2 Why does a person from the government go to Buckingham Palace? ______

3 Who allows the Lords to sit down? ______

4 Where do the MPs stand in the House of Lords? ______

5 Who writes the Queen's Speech? ______

6 How long is the Speech? ______

7 What is the Speech about? ______

d) 04 Listen to the second part again. Put the pictures in the right order.

3 Exploring Trafalgar Square ➜ SB (p. 11)

a) There is so much more to see at Trafalgar Square. Use the phrases in the box for internet research. Then write descriptions of the Trafalgar Square sights where Alyssa has been.

> 51.5 metre-high monument • north/west/north-east/centre of the square • one of UK's most important historical figures • cultural icon and symbol of friendship • four animals • gift from Oslo every December • High Commission building • red and white flags • jazz concerts in the evening • story of European art • café in the crypt[1] of the church • Nelson Mandela: 1996 • each: 7 tonnes

Canada House

This High Commission is a magnificent building to the west of Trafalgar Square. It is famous for its red and white flags.

Lion sculptures

National Gallery

Christmas tree

South Africa House

St Martin-in-the-Fields

Nelson's Column

b) Use the information in a) to draw a map of Trafalgar Square in your exercise book.

c) Find pictures on the internet that show the sights on Trafalgar Square. Print them and glue them in above.

d) Which two sights would you like to see at Trafalgar Square? Give reasons.

e) Write two descriptions like in the example for sights that you know in London. Present them in class.

[1] crypt [krɪpt] *Krypta*

4 WORDS The Commonwealth ➜ SB (p. 12)

LERNEN

Alyssa is Canadian, so she is from a Commonwealth country. Fill the gaps in the following text about the Commonwealth. The information in brackets ( ) may help.

The *Commonwealth of Nations* was founded in 1931. It is a group of 53 (1) member (= part of) states, most of which were colonies in the (2) era (= time) of the British Empire and want to continue to share a (3) diplomatic relationship with the United Kingdom and other Commonwealth countries. It is home to 2.4 billion people and was founded to promote world (4) peace (≠ war), democracy[1] and liberty and to fight against racism[2], poverty[3] and disease. Leaders of Commonwealth countries meet (5) face to face (= in person, personally) every two years to discuss shared (6) goals (= things they want to achieve), (7) they give (= present) their opinions and (8) consult (= talk and try to agree) with one another. The (9) organisation (= group of member states) has its own flag, anthem and even a version[4] of the Olympics – the Commonwealth Games – which take place every four years. Queen Elizabeth II is the Head of the (10) Commonwealt (= organization of states).

5 Schools say no to phones ➜ SB (p. 12)

French children under the age of 15 are not allowed to have a mobile phone at school any more (except for in emergencies[5]). 70 % of British adults believe a similar law should be introduced in the UK.

a) What do you think? Are the French and the British right? Think of at least four reasons why children should not have phones in school and four reasons why they should.

Why children **should not** have phones in school	Why children **should** have phones in school

b) Work with a partner and prepare a short dialogue based on your answers in a) on the reasons why children should (not) have phones in school.

Partner A: *I think mobile phones make it difficult to concentrate in class.*

Partner B: *I don't ...*

[1]democracy [dɪ'mɒkrəsi] [2]racism ['reɪsɪzəm] *Rassismus* [3]poverty ['pɒvəti] *Armut*
[4]version ['vɜːʃn] [5]emergency [ɪ'mɜːdʒənsi] *Notfall*

6 REVISION Silent disco (Simple past) ➔ SB (p. 13)

In an email Alyssa writes about the silent disco in the Shard. Complete her email with verbs in the simple past.

be (2 x) · finish · go · hear · know · love · message · not go · not visit · say · take · tell

Hi Judy!

How's things? Last week I really, really wanted to go to the silent disco in the Shard! But we (1) ____________ because we (2) ____________ too young – it's over-18s only. (3) ____________ (you) the Shard is the tallest building in Western Europe and overlooks London and you can take in lots of the sights? Well, we can go the year after next because it looks like lots of fun! My friend James (4) ____________ me the other day because he (5) ____________, and (6) ____________ me it (7) ____________ amazing. He could only go for four hours because it (8) ____________ at 2 am, but he (9) ____________ the atmosphere. He (10) ____________ it was funny when he (11) ____________ off his headphones because all he (12) ____________ was people singing! (13) ________________________ (your brother) something similar in Toronto? Write soon! Al xxx

7 REVISION St Martin-in-the-Fields (Simple present and simple past) ➔ SB (p. 13)

Complete Alyssa's messenger chat with her cousin Sylvan about her visit to St Martin-in-the-Fields. Use the correct verbs and tenses. Some verbs are given in the box. You may add more words if you need to.

appear · not be · can · eat · enjoy · have · hold · love · need · organize · see · sound · want · watch

Alyssa: Yesterday ________ so weird! We ________ to a church, but it ________ a really cool one.

Sylvan: That ____________ really boring!

Alyssa: Nope! It's called St Martin-in-the-Fields and it ______ on Trafalgar Square. But it ________ a café underground in the crypt! ________ that creepy[1]?!

Sylvan: Hahaha! That's mad! ______________ there? What ______________?

Alyssa: I ____________ lasagne, and Mom and Dad ____________ soup (like always!).

Sylvan: So it ____________ just a café then?

Alyssa: No, they ____________ jazz events on Wednesdays and ____________ concerts some lunchtimes. And remember when we ____________ "Sherlock"? It even ____________ in that too!

Sylvan: I really, really ________ to go there now! I ________ to visit places that I ________ in films and on TV!

Alyssa: Yes, we all ____________ it there. Maybe you ____________ come and visit me in London, then we can go!

Sylvan: Yes, please! Right, I ________ to go – got football practice in half an hour. See you!

Alyssa: Catch you later, cous'!

[1] creepy ['kri:pi] *unheimlich, gruselig*

8 Words that run together ➔ SB (p. 14)

a) Look at the following phrases from a conversation and decide who said them: tourist (T) or tourist information worker (W).

1 The best way to see London is on one of its buses. ☐

2 I've heard I can take an official tourist bus, but do some of the normal lines take you around the sights too? ☐

3 You should have visited London in August if you wanted to see the Notting Hill Carnival. ☐

4 A few of my friends came last year and told me I would love it. ☐

5 All you need is an Oyster Card or contactless card. ☐

6 Remember you are not allowed to pay with cash any more. ☐

7 It is a lot more fun if you sit upstairs at the front of the bus! ☐

b) 05 Listen to the recording. Underline the words in a) which run together and are pronounced as one.

c) ● Alyssa's dad goes back to the London Tourist Office for more information and help. With a partner, use the information below for a conversation between the tourist worker and Alyssa's dad.

d) 06 Listen to the conversation. Note down phrases that you find useful in your exercise book.

e) Practise the conversation again. Try to use phrases from the recording. You can record yourself too.

9 South London ➜ SB (p. 17)

a) Read the following text about South London. Give each paragraph a title and write 2–3 sentences to say what it is about. You can underline key words. Write in your exercise book.

What and *where* is South London?

Seems an easy question, right? Where do you think South London is? Everything below the Thames? No? How about what the map says? No? OK then, how about all the postcodes beginning with "SE" and "SW" (all the "South-East London" and "South-West London" postcodes)? Well, postcodes SW1–SW10 are located *north* of the river. So there doesn't really seem to be any consensus where the south begins. And why do North Londoners seem to think that South London is not just a different side of the shore, but actually a whole different world?

Some areas everyone *does* agree on being in South London are Brixton, Southwark[1], Lambeth and Greenwich[2] – the capital's most ethnically diverse boroughs, especially for the Black African, Black (or Afro-)Caribbean and European populations. The streets are filled with aromas from different cuisines, hundreds of accents, dialects and languages and people coming together to trade, buy and sell, just like they have done for centuries. And they cross the river over 30 different bridges which link north and south.

But travel is a little difficult in South London – everyone knows but nobody really understands why almost no underground was built south of the river. Look at a Tube map and it seems like one half of the city was forgotten. Well, there are two good reasons: one historical, one geographical.

Historically, the important settlement of Londinium was located on the north bank of the river, and so was/is Westminster. While the north grew and grew over time, the south remained not much more than a series of small villages. On top of that, more people settled in the north (5 million) than the south (3 million). Geographically, underground lines can be built much more easily in the clay of the north bank than the sandy earth of the south. However, there are plenty of train stations (known as "overground" – so opposite to underground) which will help get you from place to place.

So South London is like a collection of small villages? It is said to combine the best of urban and rural worlds, from tall and modern buildings like the Shard and City Hall to parks and open areas like Greenwich and leafy Richmond. Brixton and Southwark are full of great places to eat and dance the night away, Greenwich (famous as the "home of time") and Wimbledon (one of the biggest sports events of the calendar) draw the visitors and Crystal Palace is picturesque and even has dinosaurs! It might not be the home of the biggest museums or Royal buildings, but there's definitely something for everyone on the "other" side of the Thames!

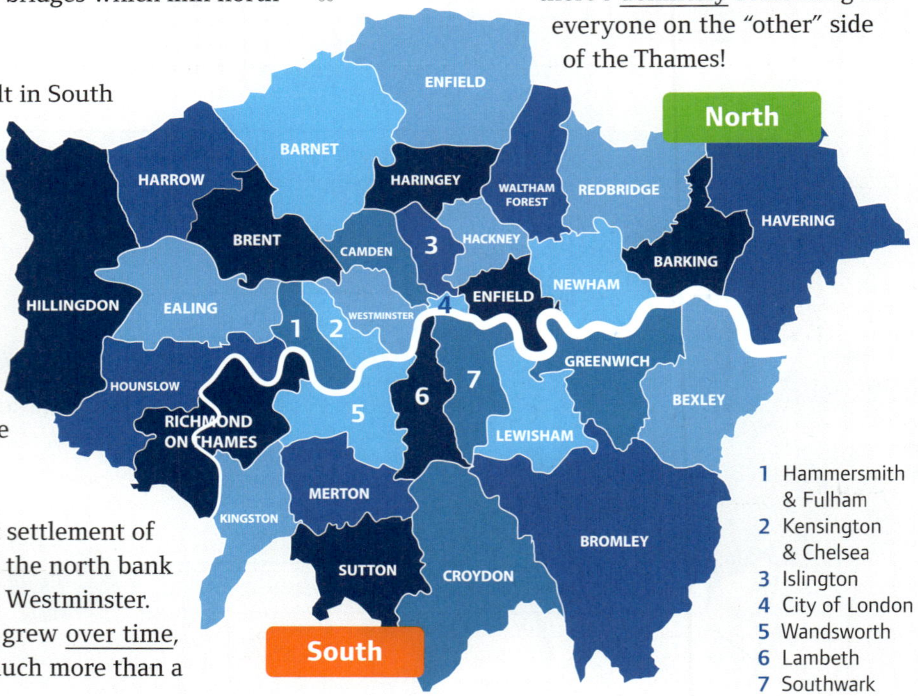

b) Using your notes and other materials, prepare a two-minute presentation on "What and where is South London?".

TIP: Look at SF 22: *Giving a presentation* on p. 132 of your student's book.

c) Look at the underlined words. Can you work out what they mean? What strategies do you use to understand them? Check with a dictionary.

[1]Southwark ['sʌðərk] [2]Greenwich ['grenɪtʃ]

10 The pull[1] of London (Listening for detail) ➔ *SB (p. 18)*

a) 07 Listen to Clàudia, Mike and Yazid, three new Londoners, talk about their experiences in their new hometown. Read the tasks first. Then listen to the text and do the tasks.

1 Match the people to the countries.

Clàudia | Mike | Yazid

USA | Syria | Spain

2 Why does Clàudia like working at the cafè? Name at least two aspects.

3 Underline the correct answer.

- Lots of people think London is **an unfriendly / a welcoming / a foreign** place.
- There is a great **community[2] / village / culture** in South London.

4 What do Mike and Yazid say about community feel in South London? Name at least three aspects.

5 What do they say about the diversity in South London boroughs?

6 What do they say about the cost of living in London? Name at least two aspects.

7 Underline the correct answer.

Clàudia sees herself **moving back to Barcelona / having a family in London / starting a business** in the future.

b) 07 Listen again. Use six adjectives from the box to describe how Clàudia, Mike and Yazid feel. Give reasons.

angry · bored · glad · hopeful · kind · nostalgic · patriotic · proud · relaxed · sad · scared

	Adjective	Reason
Clàudia		
Mike		
Yazid		

[1]pull [pʊl] *Anziehungskraft* [2]community [kə'mjuːnəti] *Gemeinschaft, Gemeinde*

11 London – the non-stop city (Passive: simple present) ➔ SB (p. 18)

You read in a magazine that there is "something for everyone" in London. Complete the sentences with one of the verbs from the box in the passive. After the gap in brackets ( ), there is sometimes further information about the negative or adverb given.

cover up · find · hold · name · overlook · play · run · suggest · transform · use

Events (1) *are held* all year round in both North and South London. A lot of these concerts, plays, markets, etc. (2) ______ (not) in guidebooks, but (3) ______ on tourist web pages. Have you heard that workshops (4) ______ (also) in community centres across the capital? One very popular event happens once a month: one of the top floors of the Shard (5) ______ into a silent disco where music (6) ______ through wireless headphones and guests can dance the night away. The area below the River Thames (7) ______ (often) as a great place to live, work and start a family. It's also a beautiful area, and the world's time system (8) ______ after the area of Greenwich in South London. Unfortunately, lots of old, traditional buildings (9) ______ (not) now because prices have gone up so much. Their doors (10) ______ (often) and you cannot see the amazing interiors from the outside.

12 Borough Market (Passive: simple present and simple past) ➔ SB (p. 18)

Borough Market is a magnet for tourists and Londoners. Find out more about it: complete the sentences with the verbs in brackets ( ) either in the active or in the passive. Use the right tense: simple present or simple past.

Borough Market, at the southern end of London Bridge, (1) ______ (found) around 1,000 years ago, although there (2) ______ (be) no official opening. For a long time it (3) ______ (use) by many Londoners because of its location – for centuries, the bridge (4) ______ (be) the only way to cross the river. People today (5) ______ (attract) by the market's history, diverse products and famous traders. But history hasn't always been kind to Borough Market – in the 1970s, the selling of food and drink (6) ______ (transform) by supermarkets and, because the market (7) ______ (not protect), it almost (8) ______ (disappear). In November 1998, a three-day 'Food Lovers' Fair' (9) ______ (organize) in the Market by Henrietta Green, a British food writer. Visitors (10) ______ (treat) to delicious food that (11) ______ (grow, prepare and cook) by 50 of the best producers in Britain. It (12) ______ (see) as a huge success. Borough Market (13) ______ (completely rebuild), and (14) ______ (be) open six days a week to visitors from around the world.

13 London facts (Passive with *by*) ➔ *SB (p. 19)*

a) All the following statements written by one of Alyssa's Canadian friends in his homework about London are wrong. Use passive sentences with **by** to correct the answers (given in brackets). Write in your exercise book. Be careful to check the tense!

1 Tower Bridge dominates[1] London's skyline. → (London Eye)
2 The city of London organized the 2016 Summer Olympics. → (2012)
3 The ancient Greeks named the city 'Londinium'. → (the Romans)
4 A bar at the top of Tower Bridge holds a silent disco once a month. → (the Shard)
5 Spanish colonies founded the Commonwealth in London in 1926. → (British)
6 The Prime Minister opens Parliament every year. → (the monarch)
7 King Charles II destroyed 13,200 houses in 1666. → (the Great Fire)
8 The Houses of Parliament look after the Imperial State Crown. → (Tower of London)

b) Write five incorrect statements about different London sights in your exercise book. Then work with a partner. Correct each other's sentences orally.

14 MIXED BAG South London walking tour ➔ *SB (p. 19)*

● Read the introduction to a walking tour for visitors around South London and fill in the gaps. The information in brackets ( ) can help you.

"Welcome to South London and the South Bank, a (1) ______________ (= not like any other) and exciting area! This part of town (2) ______________ (found) hundreds of years ago as a place of leisure outside the City of London. It (3) ______________ (be) popular with theatre fans at first, then gardens (4) ______________ (add) in the 18th century. The area that (5) ______________ (know) as the South Bank (6) ______________ (cover) around two square miles and (7) ______________ (be) now a busy outdoor public space right next to the river. It (8) ______________ (transform) by the Festival of Britain, an event which (9) ______________ (take place) in the summer of 1951. The only building from the Festival that (10) ______________ (remain) today is the Royal Festival Hall, (11) ______________ (relative pronoun) concerts (12) ______________ (still hold) regularly. The Royal Festival Hall is now part of the Southbank Centre, (13) ______________ (relative pronoun) is a large group of cultural buildings that, over the years, (14) ______________ (grow) to become the largest arts centre in the UK. The Southbank Centre (15) ______________ (be) one of the UK's top five visitor attractions for a while now. Most of the visitors here (16) ______________ (attract) by the Centre's exciting programme of events or (17) ______________ (want) to visit one of its cinemas or theatres. If you visit one of its many restaurants, you (18) ______________ (find) delish local and foreign food. Under the Centre you can see skateboarders and lots of different murals, which (19) ______________ (cover up) all the time by new graffiti artists. Now I (20) ______________ (tell) you about the many street performances here, which give the area a really fun, relaxed (21) ______________ (= atmosphere) …"

[1] dominate ['dɒmɪneɪt] *dominieren, beherrschen*

15 STUDY SKILLS Reading for detail ➔ SB (p. 20)

Read the text about a famous Londoner and do the tasks.
The tips on scanning on p. 20 of your student's book may help you.

"The Greatest Londoner of all time"

Is it David Bowie? David Beckham? Or even Elizabeth II? No. According to a survey run by the Museum of London, it is none other than award-winning[1] producer and star of nature documentaries Sir David Attenborough, famous for series such as *Blue Planet*, *Planet Earth* and *Life on Earth*.

David Frederick Attenborough was born in 1926 in London. As a child, he loved collecting fossils and stones, and went on to study geology and zoology. In an interview with TimeOut, he said, "Every child born is interested in the natural world but as life goes on some people lose it. If they do lose it altogether, they have lost something very precious[2]."

He joined the BBC in 1952 and the British public saw him for the first time ever on television in 1954. The presenter of the programme *Zoo Quest* became ill, and Attenborough had to step in at the last minute. Since then, he has become known across the world for his high-quality films on the lives of animals and plants, both on land and under the sea.

In 1979, Attenborough started work on *Life on Earth*. It would become the first in a series of nine in the "Life" series. The quality of the programmes has influenced an entire generation of film-makers and scientists, who are proud to work with Attenborough on his shows, because they know the world is a better place thanks to them. After around 20 years filming different plants and warm-blooded animals, he realized that there were two huge areas still to be covered: amphibians and reptiles. The result was *Life in Cold Blood*.

Attenborough is generally a private man. He does, however, speak loudly and often about one topic: our life on the planet and how it affects climate change. He believes one way to solve the crisis is to generate and store energy from renewable resources – if we don't take action now, the problems for the natural world will be irreversible. He loves where he lives. In the same TimeOut interview, when asked where his favourite place is on the planet, he answered simply, "Richmond, Surrey. My favourite place by a long way. Partly because I live there, partly because my friends and family are there. […] London has fine museums, the British Library is one of the greatest library institutions in the world … It's got everything you want, really."

a) Are the sentences true or false? Tick (✓) the correct answer and write down the lines where you found the answer.

	True	False	Lines
1 David Attenborough likes to give interviews about his life.	○	⊗	31
2 He first appeared on TV in the UK in 1952.	○	⊗	15
3 He is recognised as a talented producer.	⊗	○	4 - 24
4 He likes Richmond because it has wonderful museums.	○	⊗	40

b) Finish the sentences in your own words. Write in your exercise book.

1 *Life on Earth* led to eight …
2 Around 1999 Attenborough had the idea for …
3 He thinks renewable energy could …
4 People who make films believe his shows help …
5 He believes all young children …
6 A London museum asked who the …

c) Write short answers to the questions. Write in your exercise book.

1 Why did Attenborough appear on *Zoo Quest*?
2 Why did he make a programme about amphibians and reptiles?

d) Imagine you are a wild animal. Describe what happened when David Attenborough and his team came to film you for a programme. Write about 200 words in your exercise book.

[1] award-winning [əˈwɔːd wɪnɪŋ] *preisgekrönt* [2] precious [ˈpreʃəs] *kostbar, wertvoll*

16 Writing a formal email ➜ SB (p. 21)

a) Which of the following statements are right (✓) and which are wrong (✗) when writing a formal email?

1 You should use long forms (I will, we have, etc.) and not short forms (I'll, we'll, etc.). ◯
2 The subject line should be short but contain information on the content. ◯
3 It's better to write 'oe', 'ae', 'ue' and 'ss' instead of 'ö', 'ä', 'ü' and 'ß' in names, e. g. 'Heinrich-Boell-Strasse'. ◯
4 You should include your postal address at the top on the right. ◯
5 You should add a few extra people in copy ('cc') to make sure your email arrives. ◯
6 You should always start an email with "Dear Sir or Madam," or with the person's name. ◯
7 You should avoid informal language like 'cool' and 'brilliant' as it looks unprofessional. ◯
8 Try to use many "!!!" and "???" in your emails to show how important everything is. ◯

b) Finn has received an answer from the *Black Cultural Archives* telling him that the musician Masego Kinch would be happy to help with the project. Write Finn's email to Masego Kinch. Remember to say where you got his name and ask for help with your project.

Finn's notes for his email:
– explain who I am and why I'm writing
– short description of my project
– conclusion and thanks
– *Black Cultural Archives*
– contact person
– ask for help

17 WORDS A crossword puzzle ➜ SB (p. 22)

a) ○ Write the answers in the puzzle and find the word in the blue boxes.

1 a moving set of stairs
2 someone who works but doesn't get paid
3 to take place
4 a series of rules decided by an organization
5 to remember an event
6 same as *thankful*
7 to wish you hadn't done something

The word down means: You need to be very fit to be one.

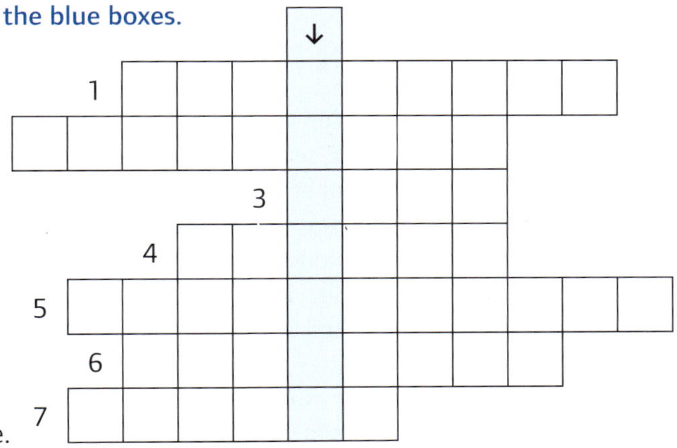

b) Use some of the words to complete the following welcome from the tour guide to *The Monument*.

"I'm really sorry there's no (1) __________ or lift to get up The Monument – I'm afraid we'll have to go up on foot. Sometimes I feel like an (2) __________ climbing those 311 steps at least 5 times a day! As we all know, The Monument (3) __________ the Great Fire of London, which took place in 1666. We're (4) __________ to all the (5) __________ who give up their time to show visitors around and help you have a lovely time here in our beautiful city!"

18 MEDIATION COURSE Das kaputte Walkie-Talkie ➔ SB (p. 23)

a) ○ Alyssa fand folgenden Artikel über das *Walkie-Talkie*. Sie bittet dich um Erläuterungen, da sie nur etwas Deutsch spricht. Lies Alyssas Nachricht und unterstreiche, was sie wissen möchte oder nicht verstanden hat. Gib jedem Gedanken eine Zahl.

This is so cool! They're writing about my favourite building in London in German magazines now! It's great everyone loves the Walkie Talkie! I'm surprised it's 220 metres tall – that must make it taller than St Paul's. But didn't I read somewhere they changed it? And now it's 'top-heavy' and dangerous and like an airport design. Is that right?

What does the Walkie-Talkie have to do with a jaguar from the zoo? What happened? Did the owners of the zoo have to pay £1,000?!

So, it won a magazine building design award too for being the best new building? The architect must be really proud! See! Told you it was amazing!

b) ○ Lies nun den Artikel und finde die Antworten auf Alyssas Fragen bzw. korrigiere ihre falsche Annahmen. Unterstreiche die richtigen Antworten und schreibe die entsprechende Zahl für jeden Gedanken in a).

Das kaputte Walkie-Talkie

20 Fenchurch Street – auch als *Walkie-Talkie* bekannt – hat seit seiner Fertigstellung im Jahre 2014 und der Eröffnung des dreistöckigen *Sky Garden* im Jahr darauf in gleichem Maße sowohl für Aufruhr als auch Erstaunen gesorgt. Seine 38 Etagen ragen 160 Meter in die Londoner Skyline, jeder erkennt seine einzigartige „kopflastige“ Form. Von den einen gehasst, von den anderen bewundert: Die Probleme, mit denen das zwölfthöchste Gebäude im Großraum London seit Öffnung seiner Pforten konfrontiert ist, sind zahlreich.

Architektur-Blogger Oliver Wainwright beschreibt das *Walkie-Talkie*: „Man fühlt sich, als ob man in einem Flughafen gefangen sei.“ Andere wiederum betonen das Design, das mit seinen breiteren oberen Etagen wohl eher aus den Mieten Kapital schlagen soll, als dass es eine aufregende Designraffinesse darstellt. Fachleute sehen es als nichts weiteres als technischen Schnickschnack. Selbst der uruguayische Architekt Rafael Viñoly distanzierte sich komplett von dem Projekt, indem er „Da steht zwar mein Name, aber es ist nicht mein Gebäude“ äußerte.

In der ursprünglichen Planung von 2005 sollte das *Walkie-Talkie* eine Höhe von 220 Metern aufweisen und damit eines der höchsten Gebäude der Stadt werden. Ein Jahr später wurde diese Höhe jedoch reduziert, da man Auswirkungen auf St Paul's Cathedral fürchtete.

Es hatte den Anschein, dass das *Walkie-Talkie* nie errichtet werden würde – der Bau wurde aufgrund der Krise im Jahre 2008 um drei Jahre verschoben. Doch schließlich öffnete es 2014 seine Türen, nur um ein weiteres Ärgernis heraufzubeschwören: den Verbrennungsskandal. An einem besonders sonnigen Tag reflektierten die Glasscheiben des Gebäudes das Licht so intensiv, dass es sich zu einer starken Strahlung entwickelte: Teile eines in der Nähe stehenden Jaguars wurden zum Schmelzen gebracht. Das führte zu einer Entschädigungszahlung in Höhe von etwa £ 1000 an den Fahrzeughalter sowie zur Installation eines vorläufigen Schutzschildes. Dieses Problem ist nun glücklicherweise gelöst.

Zu guter Letzt war der Wolkenkratzer der nicht gerade stolze Empfänger des *Carbuncle Award*, den die Zeitschrift *Building Design* für das hässlichste Gebäude, das in den letzten zwölf Monaten im Vereinigten Königreich errichtet wurde, verleiht. Selbst Viñoly räumte ein: „Wir haben viele Fehler gemacht“.

c) Verfasse eine Nachricht an Alyssa.
Beantworte ihre Fragen oder gib ihr die Information, die sie interessiert.
Schreibe in dein Übungsheft.

19 Visiting a skyscraper (Verbs with two objects) ➜ *SB (p. 24)*

Read the sentences below to tell your friends about your visit to the Walkie-Talkie in London. Underline the correct option. Remember sometimes both will be correct.

1 My friends **gave me the nickname "bird man" / gave the nickname "bird man" to me** because I love climbing things.

2 That's why they **got us tickets / got to us tickets** to go up the Walkie-Talkie.

3 My friend Peter **sent me a text / sent a text to me** in the morning saying he couldn't come.

4 I **wrote him back / wrote back to him** saying it was fine because I know he is afraid of heights[1].

5 I **said him / said to him** it was a pity he couldn't come.

6 I **suggested my friends / suggested to my friends** that we meet at the main entrance at 11 am.

7 As we went up in the lift, I **explained them / explained to them** why people call it the "Walkie-Talkie".

8 At the top, the guide **explained to us / explained us** what the different buildings were that we could see.

20 Alyssa's parents' thoughts (Personal passive) ➜ *SB (p. 24)*

● Alyssa's parents have written an article for their local School Council about their daughter's stay in London. Complete the sentences in the personal passive. Use the information in the boxes.

also send / we / a magazine full of great special offers

give / lots of parents / expensive rooms

give / our daughter / the chance

not explain / we / how expensive the room was

offer / our family / a special price on plane tickets

promise / Alyssa / a room

show / Alyssa / another room

We were so grateful (1) that our daughter was given the chance to study in London, although I think we were more excited than she was! We were planning months in advance, and (2) Alyssa was promised a room close to the school, so we were happy! (3) We weren't explained how expensive the room was! But it's something you only do once in a lifetime, so why not? Plus, (4) our family was offered a special price plane tickets so we just had to accept! And (5) we were also sent a magazine before we flew to London, so we managed to save some money there. Well, when we were there, we went to visit the room they recommended, but we hated it. So (6) Alyssa was shown another room by a lovely lady who worked at the school and who said (7) lots of parent were given, but decided their children should live in a different place.

We're so happy we found her!

[1]be afraid of heights [hart] *Höhenangst haben*

21 PRONUNCIATION An interview (Connected speech) ➜ *SB (p. 25)*

a) 08 Do you remember Clâudia, Yazid and Mike from exercise 10 who have just moved to London? Listen to some phrases they used in the interview. Complete the following sentences.

1 So, ______________________________ all know each other?

2 It's actually an amazingly diverse place to work, and everyone ______________________ is really friendly.

3 ______________________________, ______________?

4 So, ______________________________ advantage?

5 It seems that ______________________ places in London are now too expensive for Londoners.

6 I'm ______________________________.

7 I also live in South London, so I understand ______________________________.

b) With a partner, read out the phrases as you heard them in the interview. Focus on connected speech.

22 MIXED BAG Home again ➜ *SB (p. 25)*

Read the report Alyssa wrote for her school magazine after returning from six months in the UK. Complete the sentences with the right words or phrases in the correct form. The information in brackets ( ) can help you.

I'm so grateful that I (1) ______________ (give) the chance to study abroad – only a few kids (2) ______________ (choose) for this program every year. During the first week I (3) ______________ (take) to see a lot of sights (4) ______________ my parents, and we (5) ______________ (give) so much information that my head (6) ______________ (start) to spin! They helped me to look for a room when we (7) ______________ (not – like) the one that the school (8) ______________ (find). I (9) ______________ (offer) a better room (10) ______________ a nice host family. After my parents (11) ______________ (leave), the family (12) ______________ (introduce) me to lots of people. I only (13) ______________ (= feel sad about) a couple of things now. One: I (14) ______________ (not – allow) to go to the silent disco at the Shard because I (15) ______________ (be) too young. I (16) ______________ (love) to go there if I went to London again. Two: I didn't travel much, so I still (17) ______________ (not – see) Scotland. Oh, well. Because of the sights I (18) ______________ (visit) in London, I (19) ______________ (have) a better understanding of UK history now. I'm really interested in street art now too. I (20) ______________ (tell) by friends and family that I'm good at art, so maybe I can paint a mural like Banksy!

23 TEXT Escape from Uncle Jack ➔ SB (pp. 26–29)

a) Scan the text in your students' book again and read the phrases below carefully. Then match them to one of the parts of the story.

A: lines 1–70 | **B:** lines 71–132 | **C:** lines 133–223 | **D:** lines 224–278

1 Uncle Jack is caught in the fire when a burning building collapses on top of him. C

2 Samuel and Catherine pull a large piece of wood into the water to help save them. D

3 The three friends try to escape from Uncle Jack, who finds out they are running away. A

4 They are trapped with burning houses on one side and Uncle Jack on the other. B

5 Catherine is on a roof and needs Samuel and Gideon's help to get down. A

6 Uncle Jack almost convinces[1] the children to come back to him and away from the fire. C

b) ● Look at the list of the adjectives and phrases describing people. Decide which word(s) might describe each character in the story and find the line(s) in the story to support your ideas.

not afraid · aggressive[2] · careful not to hurt others · caring · clever · fast · making sb. feel less worried about sth. · ready to do sth. dangerous · scared · scary · not telling the truth · very angry

Sam/Samuel

- clever 59
- caring 15
- fast 10
- make sb. feel less worried about sth.

Gideon

- scared 120

Uncle Jack

- angry 18
- not telling the truth 165
- scary 203–204
- aggresive 77

Catherine

- ready to do sth dangerous 75
- caring 210
- not afraid 75

c) You are a reporter for the *Pudding Lane Times* interviewing the children in the story. Use a mindmap to collect ideas for questions and possible answers. Think of at least five questions. Write in your exercise book.

You may think about: what happened after they jumped in the Thames / how they felt / what their plans were.

d) One of you is the reporter for the *Pudding Lane Times*, the other one is one of the children in the story. Practise the interview with your partner and be ready to act it out in class. Use your mindmap for the questions and answers.

[1]convince sb. [kən'vɪns] *jdn. überzeugen* [2]aggressive [ə'gresɪv]

1 Talk like a Londoner (Connected speech)

Alyssa finds it difficult to understand the Londoners. Listen to her conversation with Tom and complete the following tasks.

a) ○ 09 Which phrases do you hear? Listen and tick (✓) the correct phrases.

1 has she been	◯	6 didn't I say that	◯	11 you had better watch out	◯
2 shall I teach you	◯	7 but you said that	◯	12 show me your book	◯
3 some of the rest	◯	8 give me the butter	◯	13 Let me see	◯
4 glass of water	◯	9 that's natural	◯	14 do you want to	◯
5 fish and chips	◯	10 you are a natural	◯	15 but that's your book	◯

b) ● 09 Listen again. Underline the words in a) in which connected speech is used.

c) 10 Listen and repeat.

2 Murals around London (Listening for gist and detail)

Alyssa really liked the murals she saw in Brixton so her host brother Tom takes her to see other murals around London. First read the tasks, then listen to the text twice and do the tasks.

a) 11 Look at the pictures below. Which murals are Alyssa and Tom talking about? (Circle) the letters.

A

B

C

D

E

b) ● 11 Complete the sentences with the correct words or phrases from the text. You may need to change the form of the words.

There are many ______________________ around London. They are also called __________________.

Each of them ______________ a different story. Many show ________________, myths or fairy tales. Others are used ________________________. Some have been ___________________ with plexiglass to protect them, because sometimes murals __________________. But more often they ___________________________ by the people who own the walls or doors they were painted on because ___________________________.

3 Alyssa in Camden (Connecting information)

Alyssa went to Camden Market. She is looking at the statue of Amy Winehouse.

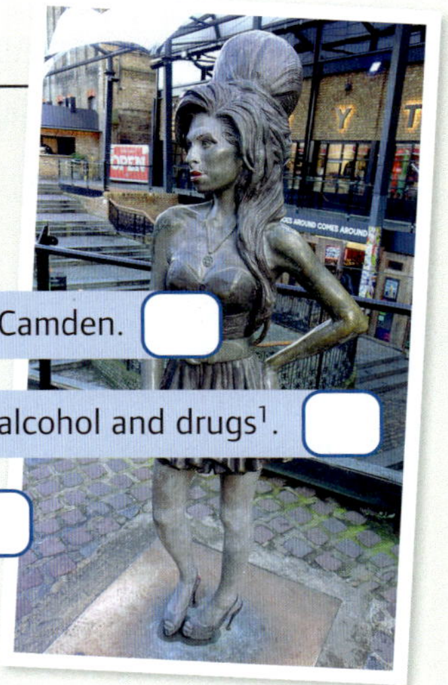

a) 12 Listen to the text. What are Alyssa and Katy talking about? Find the correct ending for sentence parts 1–7. Be careful: There are more endings than you need.

1 Amy's family
2 Amy's first job
3 Amy was discovered when she
4 The artist who created Amy's statue
5 The music programme
6 The schools' programme
7 Amy spent a lot of time

- was performing in clubs and pubs around Camden. ☐
- helps children learn about the dangers of alcohol and drugs[1]. ☐
- wanted to make her look glamorous[2]. ☐
- living and working in Camden. ☐
- was selling candles at Camden Market. ☐
- set up a foundation[3] in her name. ☐
- wanted her to look helpless and powerful at the same time. ☐
- was singing at Camden Market. ☐
- helps young people start a career[4] in music. ☐

b) ● 13 Listen to the second part of the conversation and complete the task. Listen for the numbers 1–5 below. What do they mean? Write notes.

1 1 year: ______

2 12 weeks: ______

3 2 weeks: in that time ______

4 18-25: ______

5 3 years: ______

Check: Listening

a) Vergleiche deine Antworten mit den Lösungen auf Seite 70 im Workbook.
b) Schätze deine Antworten mit einem grünen oder roten Gesicht ein.

	🙂	☹	→
1 Hast du in Aufgabe 1 gut die zusammengezogenen Wörter identifizieren können?	○	○	1
2 Konntest du in Aufgabe 2 die Sehenswürdigkeiten korrekt bestimmen?	○	○	3
4 Ist es dir in Aufgabe 3 gelungen, die Satzteile richtig zu verbinden?	○	○	3
5 Hast du in Aufgabe 3 dem Text zusätzliche Informationen entnehmen können?	○	○	2, 3

c) Wenn du dich rot eingeschätzt hast, schau dir die rechte Spalte an. Die Nummern führen dich zu den passenden Übungen im Skills Training (S. 20–21). Dort kannst du gezielt Listening trainieren.

[1]drug [drʌg] *Droge* [2]glamorous ['glæmərəs] [3]foundation [faʊn'deɪʃən] *Stiftung* [4]career [kə'rɪə] *Karriere*

1 Connected speech practice

a) 14 Listen and underline the words/phrases in which connected speech is used.

1 London girls and boys.
2 Would you like a drink?
3 If you want to find out more.
4 Shall we come with you?
5 a bottle of milk
6 You should have told me.
7 Give me that.
8 Lots of money.

b) 15 Practise the phrases in a). Use connected speech.

c) 16 Listen and write down the phrases. Then repeat the phrases.

1 ____________________
2 ____________________
3 ____________________
4 ____________________
5 ____________________
6 ____________________

2 Street art in London (Listening for detail)

17 There is a radio programme on street art in London. Read a) and b) first. Then listen to the text twice and do the tasks.

a) Are the statements **true** or **false**? Correct the wrong ones.

	True	False	
1 London has many famous galleries.	○	○	____________________
2 There is a mural of Bob Dylan in London.	○	○	____________________
3 Banksy grew up in Bristol.	○	○	____________________
4 Banksy thinks it's a good idea when his art is sold.	○	○	____________________
5 Some street artists died.	○	○	____________________
6 There are places in London where graffiti is legal.	○	○	____________________

b) Complete the sentences.

1 In London, lots of great art is found ____________________.
2 People place ____________________ and stuffed toys in front of murals of famous people to remember them.
3 Nobody knows Banksy's ____________________.
4 Banksy's murals are not only funny, they also have a ____________________.
5 Many of Banksy's murals ____________________.
6 Graffiti is ____________________ in the UK.
7 Sometimes murals are put ____________________.

3 Amy Winehouse in Camden

18 Katy takes Alyssa for a walk around Camden. Read a) and b) first. Then listen twice and do the tasks.

a) Where do they go? Number the places shown on the map in the correct order.

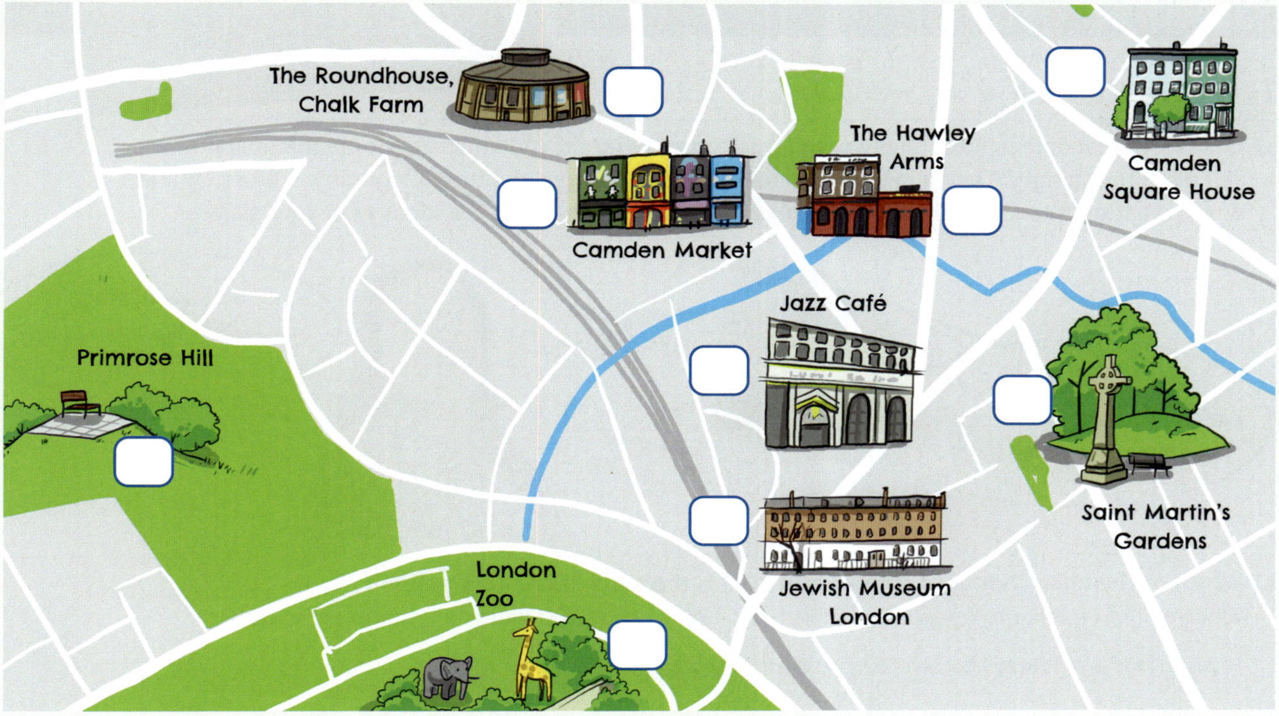

b) Look at the places that Katy and Alyssa visit. Complete the table. What can you say about the atmosphere? Choose an adjective from the box. What makes these places special? Write notes.

busy · calm · excited · lively · noisy · relaxing

Place	Atmosphere	What makes these places special?
Primrose Hill		
Jewish Museum London		
The Hawley Arms		
Camden Square		
The Roundhouse, Chalk Farm		
Camden Market		
London Zoo		

c) This is the sign that has been stolen 14 times in the past six years. Imagine your favourite rock or pop star had lived here. What would you write? Write at least two sentences. Think of: their music, life, friends, concerts you've seen, etc. Write in your exercise book.

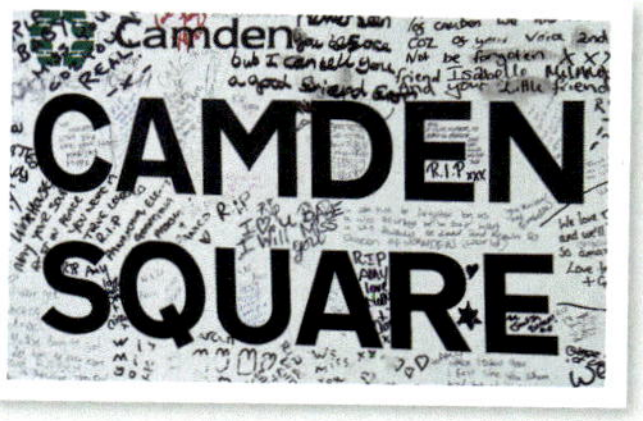

Canada

1 Life in Canada ➜ *SB (p. 39) • Wordbank 3, 4*

a) ○ Ask three people in your family or older friends: "What do you know about life in Canada? Tell me three things." They might talk about sports, languages, politics, geography, culture, animals or the weather. Make a table and write down who said what. Share the ideas with your class.

Lots of Canadian kids play ice hockey, but football is even more popular there.

English and French are both official languages in Canada.

b) Which of the ideas that your class shared in a) is the most interesting to you? Why? What would you like to know about this topic? Write about 50 words in your exercise book.

I think the most interesting idea is that … because …

c) Look at the photos and read the information. Where would you prefer to go on an exchange? Why? What could you do there? How would life there be different to your life at home? Make notes and discuss with a partner.

1

Toronto
- about 3 m people
- main language: English
- very multicultural
- many film festivals, markets, art galleries, museums (e. g. hockey), theatres
- street art and modern buildings
- world's third-largest tower
- average temperatures 26 to –7 °C

2

Quebec City
- about 530,000 people
- main language: French
- some of North America's oldest streets
- Château Frontenac (hotel)
- Winter Carnival
- aquarium with polar bears, seals, etc.
- First Nations culture at Wendake
- average temperatures 25 to –17 °C

3

Nunavut
- about 40,000 people
- official languages: Inuktitut, Inuinnaqtun, English and French
- many islands
- a young population
- hunting, fishing, whale watching, camping, climbing
- local events and festivals
- traditional art
- average temperatures 12 to –32 °C

Photo 1/2/3 shows …
I would like to go on an exchange to … because …
I could go/try/learn/see …
I think life there would be quite/very different to my life at home because …

2 Messages for Lauren ➜ SB (pp. 40–41)

Lauren has asked her blog readers to leave her voice messages that she can use to make a podcast about the trip. Read a) to c) first. Then listen twice.

a) 19 What is the main idea in each person's message? Write the number of the messages in the box.

- [ ] The Beavers must work together as a team.
- [ ] The trip is a chance to learn about different cultures.
- [ ] Quebec City is a really exciting place.
- [ ] Lauren's blog is great – and useful.

b) ● Complete the table with keywords.

Question	Person 1	Person 2	Person 3	Person 4
1 Where is the person calling from?		the bus		
2 What is he/she very interested in?				
3 What is he/she worried about?				
4 What is he/she happy about?	she can get news from the blog			

c) Finish the sentences with information from the text.

1 When Kelly was fifteen she went to Quebec for a ______.

2 Gabrielle thinks that Coach is sometimes ______.

3 Brody's old team didn't take part in ______.

4 In the future, Armaan would like to work ______.

d) ● Imagine you are a reader of Lauren's blog. You are going to record a 45-second voice message for her. You can use the ideas in the box or your own ideas. Make notes and practise what you want to say. Then record your message.

talk about what you're doing now • wish the team good luck • ask about Quebec city • ask about ice hockey • give the team some tips • talk about Lauren's blog • talk about a sport that you like • talk about a bus trip that you went on, etc.

3 WORDS About Canada → SB (p. 42)

a) ○ Find the words that match the paraphrases. Write in your exercise book.

1 an area of ice for skating or hockey
2 a house that is made of ice
3 people who are living in the same place
4 a person who helps a sports team to improve
5 a leader or older person in a tribe or community
6 a way out of a room or building

b) Amelia from Ottawa has written in her diary about her new job. Find the missing words.

Well, my first day at the café is over. I'd been (1) ______________ to start this job because I love talking to people – and that's what I did all day! A reporter who was researching (2) ______________ sports teams asked for my opinion (I said that I prefer to play against girls only). Then a tourist asked me about Canadian food and we chatted about maktak: he couldn't imagine eating whale skin and (3) ______________! Later a young guy who looked really sad came in. I didn't ask him any (4) ______________ questions, but we talked about TV shows and he looked happier when he left. Then two government workers came in and talked until they reached an (5) ______________. "Sometimes it's easier to work here than in the office," one of them said, "And you (6) ______________ the best coffee in Ottawa, which helps!"

c) You are helping a Canadian exchange student to create a crossword for your school magazine. Write a definition or a paraphrase for the following words in your exercise book.

1 gravy | 2 tournament | 3 frosting | 4 to bake | 5 to fry | 6 primary school

d) On the first night in Quebec City, Gabrielle from the Ottawa Beavers emails her brother. Use opposites to rewrite the underlined phrases and keep the same meaning. Write the new text in your exercise book.

Hi Carter!

I've already been out on my first evening in Quebec City. Coach wasn't happy when Brody, Justin and I asked to go out, but he didn't stop us. Coach isn't a bad guy, really. It isn't difficult to get around on foot here. Our hostel is in the old town, and the best sights aren't far. First we saw Château Frontenac, Quebec's 'castle', which is actually a hotel. It's not a small, modern place – and the rooms aren't cheap. It's in the centre of the old town, not outside the city walls. We saw a group that was on a city tour, but they didn't seem interested, so I don't think it was a bad idea to walk around without a guide. It wasn't long after dinner but we weren't full, so we ate some poutine in a café. Of course, you can get it in Ottawa too, but this poutine wasn't the same. Justin thinks everyone here eats poutine all the time, but I don't think that's a fact. We didn't understand the people in the café. They weren't speaking formal French. It was different to what we learn at school. When we got back to the hostel a few minutes ago, the lights weren't on any more and the corridors weren't busy. We're in the game room, but I'd better go to bed.
Speak soon!

Gabrielle

Coach wasn't happy – Coach was unhappy; he didn't stop us – he let us go.

4 REVISION Antoine will probably … (Conditional sentences type I, II and III) ➜ SB (p. 42)

Find out more about Antoine. Complete the conditional sentences in the text in a way that makes sense. Use the verbs from the box in the correct form.

be (2 x) • come (2 x) • get • know (2 x) • lose • meet • practise

Antoine will probably get nervous if the other teams (1) *are* really good. He just needs to remember that the Granby Tigres (2) ______________ here if they weren't also a strong team. They have practised a lot. And if Antoine's team (3) ______________ to the final, his mother (4) ______________ to watch the game. That would be great. He would feel better if (5) ______________ that he had somebody there to support him. But even if the Granby Tigres (6) ______________, Antoine will be happy that he came to Quebec. That's because he (7) ______________ Nukilik, Lauren and the others if he (8) ______________ here. But if (9) ______________ about the game room, he (10) ______________ foosball too!

5 What should we do about tournaments? (Modal verbs) ➜ SB (p. 43)

a) Jonas is writing ideas for an article for a teen magazine about sports tournaments. He thinks that they put pressure on young people. Write the article in your exercise book so that it expresses support for Jonas' opinion. Use modal verbs.

- understand: competitions = put a lot of pressure on young people
- life = already be hard for teens : tests, homework, personal challenges
- why even harder with sports competitions?
- in our culture: always push people to be better
- sports = be a way to simply relax + have fun
- serious all the time?
- our teen years = time to learn, get to know ourselves better and enjoy all the amazing things that life offers
- use the time for boring and difficult sports practice and competitions that don't really mean anything?

TIP: You can use the verbs *must*, *need*, *should*, *can* and *may* in positive and/or negative forms.

b) You need to write an article for your English class: "Sports tournaments are bad for our planet. What can we do about this problem?" Write about 150 words. Use at least eight modal verbs (both positive and negative forms). You can use the ideas in the box or your own ideas.

be serious about sports • change the way we think about what 'successful' means • do nothing • fly to other countries • give up • go by train • just do what we want • leave the planet's problems for the next generation • only compete in tournaments close to home • play for fun, not to win • see sports as a way to have fun • stop all tournaments • travel to different cities • use our free time to help our communities and the earth

Some sports tournaments may be bad for the planet, but I believe that there are many things that we can do. We needn't stop all tournaments, but …

6 REVISION Since when has Panuk had a dog? (Present perfect simple with *since/for*) ➔ SB (p. 43)

a) Read the information about Nukilik's father, Panuk. Then use the ideas in the box to ask your partner three questions about Panuk using the present perfect simple with *since* or *for*.

have a dog • know how to build a website • own a mobile phone • play chess • be Tapeesa's friend • wear glasses

In summer 2007 Nukilik's father, Panuk, started to play chess. Almost a year later, in August 2008, he got his first pair of glasses, while in May 2014 he got a dog. Panuk finally bought a mobile phone in January 2015 and in winter 2017 he learned how to build a website. In March 2020 Panuk first met his friend Tapeesa.

A: Since when has Panuk had a dog? *B: He has had a dog since May 2014.*

b) Write facts about yourself on a piece of paper, e. g. where you live. Swap your lists. Ask each other questions using the present perfect simple with *since* or *for*.

7 Nukilik dreams about the final game (Subject-verb agreement) ➔ SB (p. 43)

A classmate has written a text from Nukilik's point of view. Underline the mistakes she has made with subject-verb agreement. Then write the correct phrases in your exercise book.

The score's 4:4. The maths are simple – we need a goal in the next minute. But it's not easy. Suddenly, I get the puck. The crowd is silent. I shoot. "Only a minority still thinks the Beavers can win now!" says the commentator. And then … GOAL! The band lifts their different instruments to play our song. Some of my team cries; some laughs. The prime minister is here. The police is guarding him. "Tomorrow will be a national holiday!" he cries, "Politics aren't important. Economics are something we can discuss another day. The government don't need to work tomorrow. The news that the Kuujjuaq Bears have won are all that Canada cares about!" Then I wake up.

8 THE DIGITAL COMPASS Internet research ➔ SB (p. 44)

a) ○ You are doing internet research for a school project. Write the keywords that you would use for each topic in your exercise book.

1 Your class is studying the aurora borealis. Your English teacher has asked you to find out which part(s) of Canada visitors who want to see these lights should go to.

2 For a class project you are researching different animals in Canada. You want to find out whether beavers would bite you or hurt you in any other way if you approached them in the wild.

3 You are working on a project about Canada's Inuit population and their way of life. You want to know more about the old stories that they have been telling for many generations.

Type your keywords from each topic into a search engine. If your keywords didn't give you useful results, change them and do the searches again.

b) ● Choose the website descriptions that look most useful. Are the websites reliable? Copy the table into your exercise book and complete it. You can use Skills File 18 on p. 130 in your student's book.

topic	website name	reliable website?	how I know that it's reliable	Is the website useful for the project in a)?
aurora b.	*Westjet Magazine*	*yes*	*– Westjet is a big Canadian company*	*yes*
…	…	…	…	

c) Share your table with a partner. Discuss what you could do better to find more reliable results.

9 Writing better texts ➜ *SB (p. 45)*

a) *Adjectives, adverbs, linking words, relative clauses* and *time markers* can all make your texts better. Copy the table into your exercise book and put the words or phrases from the box into the correct column.

TIP: Be careful: there are two words that can each go in two columns!

adjective	adverb	linking word	relative clause	time marker
personal	mostly			

after that • and • as • because • but • carefully • fast • friendly • in June • in the 1990s • magnificent • mostly • next year • personal • pretty • really • that we don't know well • that were really scary • unhealthy • unique • very • well • which we saw yesterday • who spoke loudly

b) In your exercise book, write 150 words about something interesting, scary or exciting that happened to you. Use at least two words or phrases from each group above in your text. Underline the expressions. Then swap with a partner and give each other feedback. Skills File 5 on p. 120 in your student's book may help you.

10 STUDY SKILLS Writing a comment ➜ *SB (p. 45)*

a) Complete the text about writing a comment with words from the box. There are three more words than you need.

anything • body • conclusion • expressions • facts • ideas • internet • introduction • lists • opinion • paragraphs • questions • solution • statistics • structure • topic • website

A comment expresses your (1) opinion about a topic.

Before you write (2) ______________, you should think about the (3) ______________ and collect some (4) ______________. Write two (5) ______________: things that you have experienced and any (6) ______________ that you have. Then, research the topic on the (7) ______________. A comment should always have the same (8) ______________: first, you should state your topic and opinion in a short (9) ______________. In the main (10) ______________, you should back up your main ideas with (11) ______________ and other (12) ______________. Your (13) ______________ should repeat your opinion and suggest a (14) ______________.

b) Look at the guidelines for a good argumentative text structure on p. 45 of your student's book. Do you think that the text below includes all the points? Write notes in your exercise book.

Schools are very important, because young people spend a lot of time there: Canadian teens spend about 190 days, or 1,330 hours, in class every year. With 13 years of formal education in Canada, that is a total of about 2,470 days, or 17,290 hours at school per student. You can certainly become bilingual in that time. But many students are taught in one language only. In Canadian law, the English and French languages are just as important as each other. But that does not always seem to be true in schools.

The problem with Canadian schools is that they have different language rules in different regions. It is possible to have classes that are taught in French in places with many French speakers, but not in regions with few French speakers. If we were all bilingual in English and French (and could understand some of Canada's other languages), there would be a lot more understanding between different groups of people. A bilingual education has many personal advantages for students too.

That is why all Canadian schools should be completely bilingual. The question is, how to make this happen.

11 Young Canada Radio ➜ SB (p. 47)

Danielle and Syed are presenting their popular radio show. Read a) and b) first. Then listen twice.

a) ○ 20 Which description is correct? Write the correct letter in your exercise book.

A Two teens phone the show to talk about their experience of education programmes in Canada.

B Danielle and Syed talk to teens who no longer go to 'normal' high schools.

C Two teens talk about the unusual education programmes that they have chosen.

b) Write short answers in your exercise book.

1 How long will Erin spend at her new school?
2 Name two school subjects that she'll study this year.
3 What new skill does Erin want to learn?
4 How much did Erin's family pay for the new school?
5 Name two outdoor activities that Shen does on the farm.
6 What does Shen dislike about his high school?

c) Would you like to take part in one of the programmes from the radio show? Why (not)? What aspects might you like or dislike? Write about 150 words in your exercise book.

I would like to take part in Erin's programme, because it sounds …

12 It seems to me that … ➜ SB (p. 47) • Wordbank 3

Prepare and give a three-minute talk on one of the topics below.

– Sports competitions and tournaments put too much pressure on young people.
– Sports are not just healthy: they also help us to become better people.

a) Think about your opinion and your own experience or that of people you know. You can use ideas from exercise 5 on p. 25. Then do some research online: look for facts and statistics about your topic. The information on p. 44 of your student's book may help.

b) Look at Wordbank 3 on p. 68 to find useful phrases for expressing opinions.

c) Make notes, practise what you want to say, then give your talk.

13 What has been done for Canada's polar bears? (The present perfect passive) ➜ SB (p. 48)

Lauren and her friends are playing foosball and listening to the radio. They hear a short report about polar bears.

a) Complete the text with the correct forms of the present perfect passive of the verbs in the box.

> agree • consult • do • look after • make • organize • start • study • watch • write

Many people believe that quite a lot (1) *has been done* recently to help Canada's 17,000 polar bears. A plan (2) ______________ nationally, and new projects (3) ______________ to help the bears. Many articles (5) ______________ and a film (6) ______________ about the problem. The areas where polar bears live (7) ______________ to better understand how the melting ice is affecting them. Polar bear populations (8) ______________, and Inuit experts (9) ______________. And, of course, polar bears (10) ______________ by zoos and aquariums. However, a protest (11) ______________ in Ottawa by groups that think that we need to do more.

b) ○ 21 Listen and check.

14 News from Brody (Present perfect or present perfect passive) ➜ SB (p. 48)

a) Read Brody's email to his mother. Complete the text with the present perfect or present perfect passive form of the verbs in the box.

close • describe • give • not beat • not find • not invite • not respect • take

Hey Mom!

We have our final game tomorrow! We've been busy, but Lauren wrote a blog post today, so the readers back home are probably happy now that they (1) *have been given* some news.
Not much is happening today. Maddie is angry because her new rule about smelly socks in the girls' room (2) __________. Yuck! Gabrielle and Justin are not happy, as Antoine (3) __________ them to Granby. I think he probably just forgot. Gabrielle is also unhappy because her gloves (4) __________ from the dining room. I hope someone will find them. What else? Oh yeah, Nukilik is worried because we (5) __________ his missing phone yet. But it might be in the game room – we can't look in there because it (6) __________.
You asked about Coach: well, he's very proud today because the people who are organizing the tournament (7) __________ our team as excellent. 🙂 We're playing the Granby Tigres tomorrow. They're really excited because they (8) __________ yet. But there's a first time for everything!

Love, Brody

b) Imagine you have just come back from school. Is everything the same as it was when you left? Write six sentences about any changes you notice.

Example: *The breakfast dishes have been washed. / The dog has been fed.*

15 MIXED BAG A thief in the hostel? ➜ SB (p. 48)

Lauren and Maddie are in their hostel room. Write the missing words.

"Maddie, (1) __________ (you, see) my rucksack? I can't find it," says Lauren. "I (2) __________ (leave) it on your bed this morning. I think someone (3) __________ (steal) it!" replies Maddie. The girls meet Nukilik and Gabrielle. Nukilik thinks his phone and Gabrielle's gloves (4) __________ (take) too. "Let's tell the manager!" The angry kids (5) __________ (run) downstairs to the manager's office. "A lot of our stuff (6) __________ (steal)!" says Lauren. "Isn't there a rule that everyone (7) __________ (modal verb) respect other people's things?" The manager looks at her. "Yes. There's also a rule that guests (8) __________ (modal verb) be careless with their own things. Our cleaners (9) __________ (just – find) a wet rucksack in a bathroom, a pair of gloves in the dining room and a phone under the foosball table in the game room!"

16 Coach gives a team talk (The passive with *may, can, should, must/mustn't*) ➔ *SB (pp. 48–49)*

a) Complete Coach's talk with the verbs in brackets ( ) in the correct form.

OK everyone. Can you all hear me? Good. Someone asked me where you can put your gear during the games. Your gear (1) ______________ (keep) in the lockers. The lockers (2) ______________ (reach) through the corridor on the left of the shower rooms. Our next game is very important. We are a good team to be in the tournament, but it (3) ______________ (forget) that the Inuit team are very good too, and very strong. The next game (4) ______________ (win) if we want to do well in the tournament. Now, I've said it before, but it (5) ______________ (say) again because I've seen some players out on the ice without their helmets[1]. Helmets (6) ______________ (wear) at all times when you are out on the ice. Are you listening, Warren? Rough play (7) ______________ (use), but the other players (8) ______________ (push) in the back and your hockey sticks (9) ______________ (use) in an unfair way. The rules (10) ______________ (follow). Players (11) ______________ (send) off the ice for two minutes if they break the rules. OK. Oh, and please put your smartphones away with your gear. Videos (12) ______________ (record) inside the stadium. There is an official cameraman who will take photos and record a video of the tournament instead. The photos and video (13) ______________ (buy) after the tournament final. So you don't need to worry about taking your own photos.

b) 22 Now listen to Coach's talk and check your answers.

c) Choose a sport you know well. Imagine you are the coach of a team playing that sport. Prepare a short talk as in a) to give to your team. Practise your talk. When you are ready, you can record it.

17 What will be done? (The passive with *will*) ➔ *SB (p. 49)*

allow • answer • ask • give • hold • light up • open • send

a) Look at pictures 1–8. Complete the sentences with the verbs from the box.

1 Training ______________ in the gym this week, but on pitch number two.

2 People who make noise ______________ to leave.

3 The new leisure centre ______________ by the city mayor on Sunday at 2 pm.

4 Ottawa Beaver parents ______________ a message about the bus arrival time at Riverside High.

[1]helmet ['helmɪt] *Helm*

5

6

7

8

5 At the audition you ______________________ the chance to sing your favourite song.

6 People who arrive after 8 pm ______________________ to enter the concert, even those with tickets.

7 All your questions ______________________ in tonight's exciting final episode[1].

8 To celebrate Canada's national day on July 1st, the famous CN tower ______________________.

b) Now write sentences about the pictures 1 to 3.

1

2

3

1 ______________________

2 ______________________

3 ______________________

18 EXTRA BACKGROUND FILE Indigenous peoples of Canada → SB (pp. 50–51)

a) Which group of Canadian Indigenous people do the speakers belong to? Write them down.

1 ______________________: We live in the Arctic region of Canada. In the past, we didn't live in one place but moved around, hunting for our food. Life as part of a community is very important to my people and we have a lot of respect for our elders and ancestors.

2 ______________________: I speak a language that comes from our indigenous languages and French. That is because my ancestors are both indigenous and European. We have our own traditional music and make jewellery.

3 ______________________: My people belong to one Nation out of around six hundred and thirty-four. My people and I speak our own language. We live on land that belongs to us and have our own government – this was agreed a long time ago between the government of Canada and the leaders of my people.

b) In your exercise book, write at least two more sentences about what you have learnt about each of the three groups.

c) Work with a partner. Think about what you have learnt about Canada. How is Canada different/similar to Germany? Note down as many points as you can. Then take turns to talk about it for three minutes. Think about: geography, population, terrain and wildlife.

[1] episode ['epɪsəʊd] *Folge*

19 The final game ➜ SB (pp. 52–53)

Re-read the text on pp. 52–53 of your student's book and do the tasks.

a) Are the statements true or false? Tick (✓) the correct answer and write down the lines where you found the answer.

	True	False	Lines
1 Justin has a good sense of humour.	◯	◯	______
2 Antoine was hit while he shot a goal.	◯	◯	______
3 Antoine started a fight with Number 11.	◯	◯	______
4 Antoine's coach sent him off the ice.	◯	◯	______
5 Antoine hates to be made fun of.	◯	◯	______
6 The Tigres were fast during the game.	◯	◯	______

b) Write short answers to the questions. Use your own words. Write in your exercise book.

1 How is Lauren kind (two aspects)?
2 What does Lauren think about Number 17?
3 What does Antoine's coach think about Warren's actions?
4 When does Antoine start to feel better?

c) Look at what the students said about the final game. Why do you think they said it? Write down the reason(s) in your exercise book.

1 I don't think Antoine had a good sleep the night before the final.

2 Justin must have scored the fourth goal for his team.

3 I don't think Justin is as nice as Lauren thinks.

4 Lauren and Nukilik knew that Antoine would be hungry.

5 Nukilik must have sat behind the goal of the Ottawa Beavers team.

6 I think Nukilik thought of starting a snowball fight at the same time as Lauren.

d) Imagine you are Antoine. You have just returned to your room after the snowball fight. Write an email to your friend Lihua about what happened today and how you feel. Write about 150–200 words in your exercise book.

Hi Lihua, We played in the final today. It didn't go well …

20 In the game room (The definite article) ➔ SB (p. 54)

The kids are talking in the game room. Add the definite article where it is needed or a slash (/) if you don't need one.

Antoine: What is (1) _/_ school like in Nunavik?

Nukilik: Oh, it's fine. I think (2) ______ school in Quebec is the same for everyone.

Antoine: Do you speak French at (3) ______ school?

Nukilik: In some schools they do, but in (4) ______ school where I go, we speak Inuktitut.
But we have French lessons too. (5) ______ French teacher in our school is cool. She's funny.

[Lauren arrives.]

Lauren: I hate[1] (6) ______ rules!

Nukilik: What's wrong, Lauren?

Lauren: (7) ______ rules in (8) ______ hostel are too strict. We were playing (9) ______ music in our room and someone said (10) ______ music was too loud and we had to turn it off.

Nukilik: That's not cool. But it is after 7 o'clock. I don't like (11) ______ hostels. Camping is much better.
It's great to be under (12) ______ open sky.

Lauren: I like camping too, when there's wifi! I can't live without (13) ______ technology.

Nukilik: Ha ha. Yes, you need (14) ______ internet to keep your blog. Wasn't (15) ______ tournament cool?

Lauren: It sure was. But I'm not saying that just because my team won. I love (16) ______ tournaments.
I love meeting (17) ______ kids from different parts of Canada.

Antoine: Yeah. I think (18) ______ kids at this tournament were all cool. Except Warren.

21 Wotcha mean? (Connected speech) ➔ SB (p. 54)

a) 23 Listen to eight short recordings. The speakers are saying more than one word, but because they are speaking naturally, the words sound like one long word. How many words do you think the speakers are really saying?

1 _two_ 3 ______ 5 ______ 7 ______

2 ______ 4 ______ 6 ______ 8 ______

b) 24 Listen to another recording of the words in a) as part of longer recordings.
Write the missing words in their long form. Then try to say the sentences like the speakers.

1 _Would you_ like a drink?
2 Lauren met Alyssa ______.
3 She's eating ______.
4 I ______ scoring a goal.
5 ______ take a shower.
6 I think Antoine's a very ______.
7 Hi Nukilik. ______ play foosball?
8 You can get the keys from ______.

[1] hate [heɪt] *hassen*

22 MEDIATION COURSE A project on Inuit traditions ➜ SB (p. 55)

Du arbeitest mit Patrick, einem Austauschschüler aus Irland, an einem Projekt über Traditionen der Inuit. Lies Patricks E-Mail und den Artikel. Beantworte Patricks Fragen in einer E-Mail.

Hi,

It's great that we have to work together on the Inuit project. I looked on the internet for **Inuksuk**, like our teacher said, and I found this article. The problem is that I don't understand a lot of it. Can Inuksuk only be found in some places in Canada? Where? And I'm not sure if the article says where the name 'Inuksuk' comes from and what it means?

In Ireland, there are old stone graves called *Dolmens*, but they are all the same shape. What kind of shapes can Inuksuk be? Why are they built?

Our teacher said Inuksuk are important to the Inuit. Does the article talk about that?

And one last thing – if we went to Canada, could we visit an Inuksuk?

Thanks a million!

Patrick

Ein Inuksuk (pl. Inuksuit) oder auch Inukshuk findet man im Nordpolargebiet Kanadas. Die Bezeichnung Inuksuk kommt aus der Sprache der Inuit: *Inuk* bedeutet *Mensch/Person*. Inuksuit werden gebaut, indem Felsen und Steine aufeinandergestapelt werden. Oft werden sie in Form eines Menschen gebaut. Geläufiger sind jedoch andere Formen, z. B. eine einfache Pyramide, in eine Reihe gelegte Steine oder sogar ein großer allein stehender Stein. Die Form hängt normalerweise von der Größe und Gestalt der verfügbaren Steine und den Grund der Errichtung eines Inuksuks ab.

Bei den kanadischen Inuit hat der Bau eines Inuksuk eine lange Tradition. Tatsächlich ist der älteste Inuksuk mehr als viertausend Jahre alt. Nach wie vor ist er für die Inuit sehr bedeutsam. Ein roter Inuksuk erscheint sowohl auf der gelb-weißen Flagge der Nunavut als auch als Schullogo im Gebiet der Inuit, wie an der Jaanimmarik Schule in Kuujjuaq.

Es gibt viele Gründe, weshalb Inuksuit gebaut werden. Der Hauptgrund besteht darin, dass sie den Inuit als "Helfer" dienen. Eine der wichtigsten Möglichkeiten, in denen Inuksuit helfen, ist die eines Wegweisers.

Da die Landschaft der arktischen Tundra den Reisenden nur wenige Orientierungspunkte bietet, bauten und bauen die Inuit diese Steinformationen. Dadurch helfen sie anderen Jägern, den Weg zu finden. So kann zum Beispiel eine Gruppe von Steinen, die in einer Reihe mit dem größten Stein auf der linken Seite und dem kleinsten auf der rechten angeordnet sind, einem Reisenden mitteilen, dass er nach Osten gehen solle. Inuksuit können auch darauf hinweisen, wo Nahrung versteckt oder Nachrichten hinterlassen wurden. Ein Jäger kann eine Gruppe von kleineren Steinen am Fuße eines großen Steinhaufens so anordnen, dass er einem anderen übermittelt, wo sich ein Fluss oder Seehunde befinden.

Manche ältere Inuksuit werden in traditionellen Liedern erwähnt, die über Generationen hinweg von den Eltern an die Kinder weitergegeben werden. Diese Inuksuit werden sehr geachtet und einige dürfen nur von älteren Inuit aufgesucht werden. Hält man sich als Tourist im Gebiet der Inuit auf, so ist man gut beraten, die Einheimischen zu fragen, bevor man einen Inuksuk in der Umgebung besichtigt.

23 MIXED BAG Lauren emails her dad ➜ SB (p. 55)

Lauren writes an email to her dad. Put in the missing words.

Hi Dad,

This is just a short email before we get on the bus for home. All of my bags (1) ____________ and my room key (2) ____________ to the hostel. I didn't have time yesterday to write you (3) ____________ (= the reason was) we (4) ____________ (= have a party) and then more than a (5) ____________ (= 12 people) of us had a great snowball (6) ____________ (= battle). It has been such a (7) ____________ (= great) time here. I (8) ____________ (= find) (9) ____________ (≠ old) friends – two boys from Quebec: Antoine from Granby and Nukilik from Kuujjuaq. It was even (10) ____________ (= good ++) because we (11) ____________ (≠ lose) the (12) ____________ (= competition)! Justin shot the winning (13) ____________. It was a (14) ____________ shot because one of the Granby Tigres players, my friend Antoine, thought Justin (15) ____________ (= hit hard) him on the (16) ____________ with a hockey (17) ____________ and then (18) ____________ (= begin) a fight with him! The final (19) ____________ was 4 to 3. The tournament trophy (20) ____________ (= put for a long time) in the main (21) ____________ (≠ exit) of school, next to a photo of the whole team – including me! It (22) ____________ by everyone (23) ____________ (= Monday–Friday) day of school! Crazy! Next year I hope (24) ____________ (= boys and girls together) teams (25) ____________ (= the rules say it is OK) to play. Then this (26) ____________ (= keen) Beaver (that means me!) can show everybody (27) ____________ are just (28) ____________ good (29) ____________ boys on the ice. OK, I have to (30) ____________ (= go) to the bus now. See you later and love to Mom! X Lauren

24 TEXT Flash fiction ➜ SB (pp. 58–59)

● 25 The flash fiction stories on pp. 58–59 in your student's book are written from different perspectives. Listen to another flash fiction story and then do the tasks.

1 How does the story make you feel? Write down three adjectives to describe the story.
2 Think about the perspective. Who or what could have written the story? Explain your answer.
3 Flash fiction can be written as a story, as a poem or both. What form is this flash fiction written as? Give reasons for your answer.
4 Which picture do you think would go with the story? Why?

1

2

3

1 WORDS Opposites and paraphrases

a) You are preparing a word game for an international youth event. Find opposites for these words (single words only). Write the pairs of words in your exercise book.

1 nearby 2 common 3 daylight 4 to hate 5 awake 6 separately

b) You are creating a crossword for an international youth magazine. Write paraphrases in your exercise book.

1 to strike 2 to vacate 3 to respect 4 to joke 5 to witness 6 to recall

2 An exchange visit to Ontario (The passive with *may*, *can*, *must*, *should* and *will*)

Imagine that you're going to Ontario on an exchange visit. You receive an email from the organization. Rewrite the text in your exercise book: change the sentences into the passive. You don't need by-agents.

First steps: We will not tell you which school we will send you to until after Easter, but your local postal worker should deliver an information pack to your home in the next few weeks. You must complete the papers inside the pack and send them back as soon as possible …

Events and activities: You can enjoy many special events during the exchange. We will hold a welcome party at City Hall, for example, and we may also offer exchange students the chance to go on an expedition in Algonquin Provincial Park. You should not bring camping equipment from home, as one of our partner organizations will give you everything here in Ontario if necessary …

Rules: You must not break the organization's rules for living with host families. You may not invite guests to sleep at your host family's home, but you may bring one or two friends from school there in the evening or on the weekend. The families will not allow you to have parties. You must respect your host family's wishes at all times …

3 Writing a comment: first steps and guidelines

a) Two of your classmates have written tips about writing a comment, but not all of the tips are correct. Read the lists. Tick (✓) the tips that are correct. Rewrite the tips that are not correct in your exercise book so that they make sense.

Berhane

- ◯ To find your opinion about the topic, brainstorm some ideas.
- ◯ Organize your ideas before you write your comment.
- ◯ Online research takes too much time, so it's better if you don't do it.
- ◯ Remember: the information that you find should not change your opinion.
- ◯ Keep your introduction short.

- ◯ Choose the right search engine settings (e. g. language, country).
- ◯ Check where information comes from after you have decided to use it.
- ◯ There are few useful[1] expressions that you can use to start each paragraph.
- ◯ Give reasons for your opinion in the main body and use facts to support it.
- ◯ Don't give your opinion again in the conclusion.
- ◯ Remember to suggest a solution in the conclusion.

Zaineb

b) Think of two more useful tips for internet research and add them to the list you wrote in a).

c) Share your ideas from b) with a partner. If your partner's tips are useful, add them to your list.

[1]useful ['juːsfl] *nützlich, hilfreich*

4 Writing a comment: structure and useful expressions

Kirima from Nunavik has written a comment for her school magazine on whether gaming should be a high-school sport.

a) Decide on the right order for the sentences. Label each sentence with a number from 1 to 8 and with *introduction*, *main body* or *conclusion*.

It's my hope that in the future there will be esports teams in high schools.

Secondly, although many people don't think that gaming is a 'real job', in reality there are now gaming tournaments around the world where the prizes are worth thousands or even millions of dollars – just like in traditional sports.

For example, in 2018 the audience for esports around the world was 380 million people and it's growing.

Young people on school sports teams usually play hockey, soccer or basketball, but I believe that online gaming, or 'esports' should also be an official high-school sport.

It is often said that gaming is very different to traditional sports, but there is evidence to support the idea that the two things are very similar.

In fact, I would like to see schools where the best gamers have coaches, because this would show the world that gaming really is a sport for which you need talent and skill.

Thirdly, many people are now starting to watch esports as a hobby too.

Firstly, gamers have to work hard, improve their technique, practise and survive in a tough, competitive environment, just like athletes do.

b) Do you agree with Kirima's point of view? Should gaming be a sport at your school? Why (not)? Write at least 150 words. Use at least five of the underlined phrases above or other phrases from p. 45 of your student's book. If you mention Kirima's points, use your own words.

5 Writing a comment: an exchange year

You have been asked to write a comment for an international youth magazine. The topic is: 'Every high-school student should spend an exchange year abroad before they are 19.' Think about and research the topic, then write about 200 words. Consider your tips from exercise 3 and your phrases from exercise 4.

Check: Writing

a) Vergleiche deine Antworten mit den Lösungen auf den Seiten 70 und 71 im Workbook.
b) Schätze deine Antworten mit einem grünen oder roten Gesicht ein.

1 Hast du in Aufgabe 2 die Passivform mit *modal verbs* und *will* richtig eingesetzt? → 1

2 Hast du in Aufgabe 3 gewusst, wie man online recherchiert bzw. einen *comment* schreibt? → 2, 4

3 Hast du in Aufgabe 4 die Struktur des *comment* richtig identifiziert, angemessene Wendungen verwendet und deine Meinung deutlich geäußert? → 3

4 Hast du in Aufgabe 5 gewusst, wie man einen *comment* mit korrekter Struktur und in entsprechendem Schreibstil verfasst? → 3, 4

c) Wenn du dich rot eingeschätzt hast, schau dir die rechte Spalte an. Die Nummern führen dich zu den passenden Übungen im Skills Training (S. 38–39). Dort kannst du gezielt Writing trainieren.

1 After the tournament (Constructions with the passive)

On the bus home, Maddie from the Ottawa Beavers emails her cousin. Rewrite the text in your exercise book. Change the underlined phrases into the passive. The passive sentences don't need a by-agent.

nobody has told you > you haven't/have not been told
the tournament people have given us > we have been given

TIP: You form the passive with a form of be and the past participle of the verb: they give us … → we are given …

With passive sentences you can **describe actions without a by-agent** (without saying who is doing the action). It is often not known or not important who is doing the action.

Hey Brooklyn!

I spoke to Uncle Rick this morning, but maybe **nobody** has told you the news yet: we won! The **tournament people** have given us a big shiny trophy, which **a teacher** will put on a shelf in the main entrance at school next week, and **the school** will show our photo there too. Since we won, **a guy from 'Ottawa TV'** has asked us to go on his TV show! **He** just needs three of us for the interview. **Coach** won't choose the three lucky kids until this evening. I think **Coach** should offer Lauren the chance to do it. Coach has just sent us some special rules for the TV interview: **we** may not wear our own clothes – just hockey kit, **we** must not make silly comments about the other teams and **we** should respect the TV guy at all times. Coach just loves to tell us what to do!

Oh, guess what: Brody and Gabrielle made a great impression at the tournament. **Two national coaches** will take them to Toronto soon to play a few games with the national youth teams there. Usually, **these coaches** don't invite 'new' kids to play with the national team at this stage, so I guess they think Brody and Gabrielle are really good!

Love, Maddie

2 Internet research: watching whales

Imagine you're planning a class trip to Canada. Your teacher has asked everyone to research possible activities. You need to find out about watching whales: where/when can you do it in Canada, and how much might it cost? Is there a youth hostel nearby?

TIP: How to find useful information online:
- Think about what keywords would be best before you start.
- Use specific keywords.
- Choose only the most useful search results.
- Check who is responsible for the website that you're using (e. g. look at the 'about us' page).
- Add useful websites to your bookmarks if you want to use them again.

a) Research the topic online to find out the answers to the questions above.

b) On the computer, write the keywords that you used and copy and paste[1] the links that you decided to click on. Then write the useful information that you found. Is it reliable? How do you know?

c) Is there anything that you could do better next time? Write a few sentences.

[1] paste [peɪst] *einfügen*

3 Writing a comment: practising useful expressions

You have been asked to write a comment for an English project at school.
The topic is: 'Some people think that chess should be a school subject. Do you agree?'
Complete the tasks below in your exercise book. For each sentence that you write, use a different expression from the boxes.

1 **Introduction**
Your opinion: chess should be a school subject. Many people think it is just a game, but you think it is a great way to practise maths and to learn to think in new and different ways.
Write three different sentences that you could use as the first sentence of your comment.

> Although many people believe that … in reality • It is often said that … but … • Although chess is not an official school subject, I believe that … • I believe that …

2 **Main body**
You have found the following information online: a 2017 research project suggested that chess helps young people to improve their maths skills.
Write three different sentences that you could use to present this information.

> There is evidence to support the idea that …: a research project showed that … • A research project from 2017 showed that …, which suggests that chess … • If you look at the evidence, you'll see why I believe that …: for example, a research project from 2017 showed that … • It's a fact that …: a research project from 2017 showed …

3 **Conclusion**
Your solution: students could do chess during of one of their maths lessons at school.
Your opinion: all young people should be taught to play chess.
Write three different sentences that you could use to state your opinion again and then present your solution.

> It's my hope that in the future …, and a good way to do this would be to … • Personally, I think that …, and this would be possible if … • I think that …, and it would be a good thing if … • I believe that … and I think all schools should …

4 An exchange year: editing your text

You are going to edit the comment that you wrote for exercise 5 on p. 37.

a) Re-read your text. Does it include everything from the checklist below? Tick (✓) every step that you have completed.

1 Have you stated your topic and opinion clearly in your introduction? ○
2 Is your introduction short? ○
3 Have you given reasons for your point of view in the main body of your text? ○
4 Does the main body of your text have one or two paragraphs? ○
5 Have you used statistics or other facts to back up your main statement in the main body of your text? ○
6 Have you used some of the useful expressions from p. 45 of your student's book in your text? ○
7 Have you stated your opinion again in your conclusion? ○
8 Do you offer a solution in your conclusion? ○

b) Edit your text so that all the steps in the checklist are complete. Then swap with a partner and give each other feedback on your texts.

Faces of the Midwest

1 About South Dakota

➜ SB (pp. 66–67) • Wordbank 3

TIP: Photo 1 shows … In the background you can see … It looks … I like this photo because …

a) Choose three of the photos 1–5. Choose the words from the box on p. 67 in your student's book which you can use to describe your three photos. Look up words that you don't know in a dictionary. Write a text of about 50 words about each of your three photos in your exercise book.

1

2

3

4

5

b) ○ Work with a partner. Choose three aspects of South Dakota that you would like to learn about while you work on this unit. Make an A4 poster with your names and your three aspects. Hang your poster on the wall in your classroom. When you have finished working on this unit, look at the posters again. Which of your three ideas did you learn about?

2 WORDS A morning at Mobridge-Pollock High School

➜ SB (p. 69)

a) ○ You are playing a word game with an American exchange student. Match the verbs and the paraphrases. Then use each verb in a sentence. Write in your exercise book.

1 to honk
2 to tuck
3 to speed up
4 to slap
5 to qualify
6 to grin

- to smile a wide smile [6]
- to hit something/someone hard with a flat hand [4]
- to make a loud, short noise (car horn) [1]
- to pass a test to do something [5]
- to go faster [3]
- to put something in or behind another thing [2]

b) You are helping your cousin with his English homework. Underline the wrong word in each sentence of the text. Then write the correct word on the right.

It was only Britain and France who fought the Seven Years War. Both countries wanted control over colonies in North America, Asia, India and Africa. Britain won, and the Treaty of Paris allowed Britain to access parts of North America, as well as some islands that were important because they produced oil. The battle of 1763 declared that Native Americans could settle west of the Appalachian Mountains. However, white American settlers did not respect the mountains as the village line. Native Americans did not want to move even further west, but they were helped to do it.

~~wave~~, mainly
caribbean
~~zanada~~
sugar farms
proclamation
boundary line
forced

3 Bethany and Ashton ➜ SB (p. 70)

26 Listen to two exchange students at a school in Rapid City: Bethany from London and Ashton from Saskatchewan. Read a) to c) first. Then listen twice.

a) ○ Which statement is correct? Circle A, B or C.

A Bethany and Ashton meet at lunchtime. They talk about funny Canadian words and their plans for this evening.

B Bethany and Ashton meet after school. They talk about their experiences with American English.

C Bethany and Ashton meet after school. They talk about language and problems with their host families.

b) Finish the sentences.

1 Ashton and Bethany first met at ________________

2 When Ashton asked about the 'knapsack', the other kids ________________

3 In the future Ashton would like to study ________________

4 The word 'bunnyhug' is only used ________________

c) Copy the table into your exercise book. Write the words from the box in the column "CanE". Then complete the table with the correct words from the conversation in AE and BE.

washroom • knapsack • scribbler • runners • pants • bunnyhug • chesterfield

CanE	AE	BE
grade 11	*11th grade*	...
washroom	...	...

4 REVISION Drew and Kaya (Simple past or past progressive?) ➜ SB (p. 71)

Drew needs to talk to Kaya at school. Put the verbs from the box into the simple past or past progressive. Add more words if necessary.

ask • drink • drive • enter • give • have • hear • not hear • not listen • pull • ring • see • sit • smile • walk (2x) • want

At 7:30 Drew (1) *was having* breakfast when his dad came in and (2) ________ him the keys to his truck. Just ten minutes later Drew (3) ________ at the wheel of the truck. As he (4) ________ into the school parking lot, he (5) ________ Bobby's old Ford behind him. They (6) ________ the school building together. Just as they (7) ________ to their classroom, Drew (8) ________ Kaya. She (9) ________ water at the fountain. Drew (10) ________ over and started to talk to her. He (11) ________ her for a date on Saturday, but then the bell (12) ________, so he (13) ________ her reply. He (14) ________ to ask her again, but now she (15) ________ to him because a friend (16) ________ her into the classroom. But Drew (17) ________ anyway.

5 A different world (Adjectives used as nouns) ➔ SB (p. 71)

a) You are helping your neighbour with her homework. She has made some mistakes with adjectives used as nouns. Underline her mistakes. Write the correct words in your exercise book.

In an ideal world, the rich would not get richer while the poors got poorer: things would be fairer. The strong would protect the weak in all areas of society and sick people would be treated quickly and for free. Lucky would share some of their good fortune with those who were not so lucky, and in this way society would be better. The young and the old would learn from each other and it would be completely normal for a young and an old to be good friends. The intelligents know that age is just a number, and in an ideal world everyone would understand this.
People would also complain less: they would learn to accept the rough with smooth, focus on the positive instead of negative and look for solutions. The people of Europe – the British, the Frenches, the Irish, the Germans and everyone else – would work together even more to share and develop their best ideas. There would be less focus on new and the contemporary: people would like old objects and try to use them for as long as possible. In fact, the trendys would have the oldest things! The great about that is that it would encourage people to just enjoy what they had and not always search for the special or the unusual just to get attention from others. The realistics might think that I am describing an impossible, but I think that this kind of world could exist – one day.

b) For a writing competition, imagine you have travelled far into the future. Describe what life on Earth is like now. Use at least six adjectives used as nouns. You can use some of the words in the box or your own ideas. Write about 200 words in your exercise book.

British · competitive · cool · familiar · free · incredible · Irish · magical · nostalgic · *old* · realistic · rich · strong · unique · unusual · weird · wise · young

I have arrived in the 23rd century and life on Earth is quite different. The old seem …

6 MEDIATION COURSE Teen rules and rights ➔ SB (p. 72)

● Emily aus Rapid City besucht bald deine Schule. Markiere die Fragen der amerikanischen Gruppe in Emilys E-Mail. Lies dir die Texte auf Seite 43 durch. Fertige Notizen an. Beantworte die Fragen in einer E-Mail. Schreibe in dein Übungsheft.

Hey,
I can't wait for the exchange in Bavaria next month! Is it OK if I ask you some questions? Frau Hoffmann sent us a German flyer with rules for teens, but I (and my friends who are going on the exchange: Riley, Diego and Jace) don't understand everything. For example, we know that German kids my age (16) don't drive, but it's Jace's 18th birthday next week, and he wants to know whether he could get a car from a car-hire company in Bavaria to use during the visit. 18-year-olds can do this in some parts of the USA, but what about Germany? What are the rules? He wants the car so that he can go camping one weekend. Actually, we'd all like to go with him – is that allowed in Germany? It would be so cool! Jace will be 18 by then, Riley and I are 16 and Diego is 14. Diego asked me to ask you if he's too young to go camping without his parents or another adult – is there a rule about that in Germany?
Something that Riley wants to know is this: all the kids on the exchange are going to have lunch at a 'Biergarten' on the day before the last day of the exchange. Will we be allowed to go in if we arrive without an adult? We don't plan to drink any beer (and our school wouldn't allow it, because you have to be 21 to drink alcohol in South Dakota), but Riley is worried that we won't be allowed to go in, especially Diego, who is younger than the rest of us. Oh yeah, Riley also wants to know about the disco that's planned for the last evening of the trip. She loves dancing! We read the rules and she thinks that she and I will be allowed to stay until 10 pm, but Diego won't be allowed to go without a responsible adult. Is that right? Or could Diego go to the disco if Jace went with him? And what about going out in general – it says in the flyer that there's a rule for what time kids have to go home at night, right? But I can't understand the details. Can you explain the rule to me, please? It all seems so complicated!
Thanks so much. My next email will be in German – I promise! 😊
Emily

1 Ausgehen – Ohne Eltern unterwegs sein

Wie lange du draußen unterwegs oder bei Freunden sein darfst, unterliegt keinen gesetzlichen Bestimmungen. Wann du zu Hause sein musst, können daher deine Eltern festlegen. Sie haben die Aufsichtspflicht und können verantwortlich gemacht werden, wenn etwas passiert. Sie müssen dir aber auch ein normales Gemeinschaftsleben ermöglichen.

2 Discobesuche und Tanzveranstaltungen

Unter 16 darfst du nur in eine Disco, wenn eine personensorgeberechtigte oder erziehungsbeauftragte Person dabei ist. Ab 16 darfst du dich immerhin bis 24 Uhr in einer Disco aufhalten. Danach heißt es nach Hause gehen. Das gilt auch, wenn ein Freund oder Freundin von dir schon volljährig ist. Ausnahmen gibt es aber bei Veranstaltungen von einem „anerkannten Träger der Jugendhilfe", das sind z. B. Jugendtreffs von Gemeinden, Vereinen oder der Kirche. Dann ist allen unter 16 die Anwesenheit bis 22 Uhr gestattet, für die 16- und 17jährigen ist um 24 Uhr Schluss. Außerdem kann die „zuständige Behörde" Ausnahmen genehmigen! Es kann sich also lohnen, euch mit dem Jugendbeauftragten der Gemeinde oder der Stadt in Verbindung zu setzen.

3 Gaststätten

Wenn du mindestens 16 Jahre alt bist, darfst du dich zwischen 5 und 24 Uhr allein in einer Gaststätte aufhalten. Bist du jedoch unter 16, dann ist dies nur unter bestimmten Bedingungen ohne Begleitung einer personensorgeberechtigten oder erziehungsbeauftragten Person möglich, nämlich wenn du zwischen 5 und 23 Uhr eine Mahlzeit oder ein Getränk einnimmst. Solltest du eine Veranstaltung eines anerkannten Trägers der Jugendhilfe besuchen oder dich auf Reisen befinden, dann gelten die Beschränkungen nicht. Um jemanden abzuholen oder etwas zu fragen, darfst du jederzeit eine Gaststätte betreten, allerdings immer nur kurzzeitig.

4 Urlaub

Ab 14 Jahren darfst du ohne deine Eltern auf Reisen gehen, brauchst dazu aber die Erlaubnis deiner Eltern, die du am besten auch schriftlich dabei hast. Für Discobesuche und ähnliche Dinge gelten dieselben Bestimmungen wie zu Hause.

5 Auto mieten

Bei der Buchung eines Leihwagens ist dein Alter besonders wichtig, in der Regel musst du mindestens 21 Jahre alt sein. Gelegentlich darfst du schon ab 18 Jahren ein Auto mieten. Das gleiche gilt für die Fahrzeugklasse. So ist es wahrscheinlicher, dass du einen Mietwagen der Miniklasse oder einen Kleinwagen mieten kannst als ein größeres Auto. Beim Führerschein gibt es eine goldene Regel, die besagt, dass du diesen immer mindestens ein Jahr besitzen musst. Führerscheine, die unter einem Jahr ausgestellt wurden, werden in 95 % der Fälle vor Ort nicht akzeptiert. Bist du bereit, einen Jungfahrer-Aufschlag zu zahlen, setzen die Anbieter mitunter das Mindestalter herab. Wieviel du dafür zahlen musst, hängt jedoch vom jeweiligen Vermieter ab.

7 Standing Rock Reservation ➜ SB (p. 75)

a) ○ Write paraphrases for the following words in your exercise book.

1 site   2 to dig   3 conflict   4 farming   5 to pollute   6 bitter

b) ○ Find the opposites of these words. Don't use the word 'not'! Write in your exercise book.

1 because of   2 allowed   3 peaceful   4 settled   5 to clean   6 relaxed

c) Re-read the text on p. 75 of your student's book, then answer the questions in your own words. Write complete sentences in your exercise book.

1 Why are the hills in the middle of the reservation so special for the inhabitants?
2 Why do people of the Lakota and Dakota Nations live on the reservation?
3 What happened to young people who followed Lakota or Dakota traditions at boarding school?
4 Why had so many people on the reservation died by the end of the 1800s?
5 What did Native Americans do when they heard about the plans for the pipeline?
6 Name two problems that the pipeline has brought for people on the reservation.

8 Drew likes riding … (Gerunds as object) ➜ *SB (p. 76)*

Drew and his friends like doing different things. Use a gerund to make one sentence out of two. Leave out the adverbs (*almost, never, often, sometimes*) in your answers.

1 Drew often rides alone. He likes that.

Drew likes riding alone.

2 Bobby sometimes watches history programmes. He enjoys that.

____

3 Kaya almost never eats Aunt Jodi's frybread. She misses that.

____

4 Randall helps in the kitchen at weekends. He doesn't mind that.

____

5 The Mobridge kids go to dances in the summer. They love that.

____

6 Drew and Bobby sometimes have to do boring homework. They hate that.

____

7 Drew often cleans his dad's truck. He doesn't like that.

____

8 Kaya's cousins never hang around in town. They can't stand that.

____

9 An exchange student (Gerunds after prepositions) ➜ *SB (p. 76)*

Mel is an exchange student from Wales. Complete the text with the correct verb forms in the box. Add a preposition where necessary.

come • not know • live • learn • make • meet • not speak • see • study • *take* • try out • work

My exchange family is just great. They're talking *about taking* (1) me with them to Rapid City next month. They know that I'm keen ________ (2) Mount Rushmore and I'm interested ________ (3) about US history. I'm excited ________ (4) for the school rodeo team too. In fact, I'm thinking ________ (5) here after school. I needn't be nervous ________ (6) anybody here. I'm good ________ (7) people and ________ (8) new friends. I'm not afraid ________ (9) hard and I needn't worry ________ (10) the language. You can never get tired ________ (11) in South Dakota, where there's so much going on. I'm really looking forward ________ (12) here again in the future.

10 What you like and don't like (Mixed gerunds) ➜ SB (p. 77)

a) You are preparing your first email to your new American exchange partner. Complete the sentences with gerunds. Write the full sentences in your exercise book. Underline the gerunds in your sentences.

1 In my free time I love …
2 At the weekends I really enjoy …
3 I'm quite good at …
4 I've never been interested in …
5 When we're on holiday, I hate …
6 I don't usually mind …
7 At home I really can't stand …
8 I sometimes worry about …
9 At school I'm always keen on …
10 I'm a bit afraid of …
11 I sometimes get nervous about …
12 I'm looking forward to …

1 *In my free time I love going to the cinema with my friends.*

b) You are going to interview a partner. Write five questions using gerunds. Use the ideas from the boxes or your own ideas. Structure your questions like this:

What's the best thing about having an older sister?

best • coolest • craziest • funniest • most awesome • most boring • most difficult • most interesting • most fantastic • most special • nicest • stupidest • weirdest • worst

be a teen • (not) have an older/a younger brother or sister • live in the 21st century • go to this school • (not) wear make-up • (not) do sport • have to do homework • learn English • (not) play an instrument • (not) ride a bike • go on a class trip • not be allowed to drive yet • come from Bavaria …

Ask your partner and make notes. Then write a short text with your partner's answers.

For Lea, the worst thing about living in the 21st century is that the planet is being polluted. She thinks …

11 An email to Martha (Mixed gerunds) ➜ SB (p. 77)

Your grandmother's friend Martha from South Dakota is coming to visit Bavaria with her family: Vince, Jennifer, Alexis and Gabriel. Martha left a voicemail and asked your grandmother to send an email with tips about what to see and do. Your grandmother is nervous about writing in English, so she has asked you to help.

a) 27 Copy the table into your exercise book. Listen to the voice message from Martha and take notes about her family members and what they like.

	Vince	Jennifer	Gabriel	Alexis	Martha
What he/she likes to do	*play golf*				

b) ○ Use another line in the table in a) to write a list of places that Martha and her family might like to visit. Recommend two places/attractions for each person. You can use your own ideas and/or ideas from the box.

Pinakothek der Moderne, Munich • Zugspitze, near Garmisch-Partenkirchen • Hauptmarkt, Nuremberg • Bamberger Dom, Bamberg • Café Roma, Munich • Neuschwanstein Castle, Schwangau • Weidener Meisterkonzerte, Weiden • Augsburg Zoo • Golfclub Ingolstadt • Ammersee, Herrsching/Dießen am Ammersee

c) In your exercise book, write an email to Martha. Use at least one gerund construction for each family member. Think of a suitable beginning and ending.

Vince is interested in playing golf, so I think he'd like to go to … And as he never gets tired of visiting castles, he'll enjoy a trip to … You said that Jennifer loves …, so a visit to … would be great for her.

12 BACKGROUND FILE Native Americans, western expansion ➔ SB (pp. 78–79)

a) ● Re-read the Background File texts on pp. 78–79 of your student's book.
Match each group of people to the correct description.

A conquistadores **B** Sioux **C** Lakota **D** immigrants from Germany/Scandinavia
E Choctaw **F** European American settlers **G** US government **H** Wichita

this group took the best land away from Native Americans in the middle of the eighteenth century ☐

people from this group had new farms in the late 19th century ☐

this group once hunted on the Great Plains ☐

some of these people believed they had the right to kill Native Americans ☐

these people became nomadic by the 17th century ☐

this group changed the way that people hunted in North America ☐

these people swapped goods with colonists ☐

people from this group were forced to move west ☐

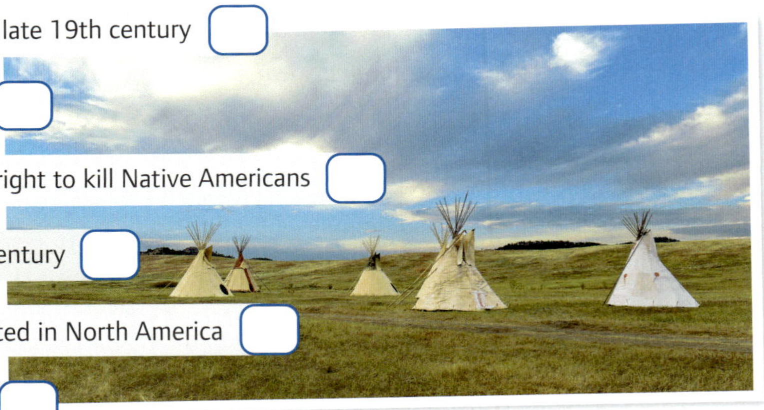

b) ● Complete the text about Native American societies of the Great Plains.

Some communities on the Great Plains were sedentary while others were (1) *nomadic*. The sedentary groups were larger and lived (2) ________ to lakes or rivers in (3) ________. They farmed squash, beans and (4) ________ and hunted animals. The groups that (5) ________ across the Great Plains were smaller, although there could be up to (6) ________ people in one group. A third kind of community combined the two ways of life: they hunted in (7) ________ and winter but also lived from (8) ________. When the conquistadores from (9) ________ arrived in North America, things began to change. Communities became more competitive because they wanted more wealth and higher (10) ________. Some groups now had guns, which led to violent (11) ________.

c) Look at the photo on p. 79 on your student's book. What does it show?
Prepare and practise a one-minute talk about the photo:

1 Describe what you can see in the photo and what is happening.
2 Say who you think the people are and where they are going.
3 Say how you think they might be feeling and why.
4 Say what you think they will do when they reach their destination.

Give your talk to your partner. Give each other feedback.

13 Kaya's diary ➜ SB (p. 80)

● A classmate writes Kaya's diary entry about Drew's visit to the rez. Read the text. Then decide whether the underlined words are correct English or not. Write the correct words on the lines on the right.

This morning, Drew was driving me out to Aunt Jodis ranch so that we could practice for the rodeo. He's very good at riding and he gave me some really good tips while we were training. He's so helpfully. I enjoyed to practice with him. Plus, I'm more confidence about making the finals. I just hope my times are as good when I will ride in front of Coach. While we were walking the horses back to the ranch, Drew has invited me to go with his family to Mount Rushmore. I was quiet surprised. I never been there before, but there's a reason for that. Before I was having a chance to answer, Cody called us. We have eaten frybread. Aunt Jodi's frybread must be the best on the whole rezervation, I'm sure of it. Drew said it was delicious. As we were eating, Cody asked Drew to come and train with her and Randall next weekend. But where will Drew be next weekend? That's right – at Mount Rushmore. Then Drew were telling everyone that I was invited to go with him. My cousins looked at each other and then at Aunt Jodi, who was looking at me. She didn't say nothing. Drew didn't notice any of this. While we was going home in Drew's dads truck, I told him we could talk about the trip to Mount Rushmore at school next week. He seemed sadly. I hate making people wait for an answer, but I couldn't tell him today. If I go with him, I know how my family will react. They'll be being so angry. And I would total understand that. They might even forbade me from going.

But if I say no, I'm not sure Drew won't understand. I'm worried about to hurt his feelings. I just don't know what to do. I wish I can talk to someone about it. Right now, keep a diary is the only thing that's stopping me from going crazy.

____

14 Tourists in South Dakota → SB (p. 81)

28 The Sutton family are tourists from California and spend their holidays in South Dakota. Read the tasks first, then listen to their conversation. You will hear the text twice.

a) ○ Tick (✓) the correct statements.

1 Mount Rushmore was finished in 1941. ◯
2 Less than 400 workers built it. ◯
3 There are more than 500 steps to the top. ◯
4 President Lincoln helped keep America together during the Civil War and ended slavery. ◯

b) ● What do the Suttons talk about? Complete the sentences with between 1–4 words into each gap.

In 1874, white men (1) ______________ in the Black Hills and the US government (2) ______________ Lakota lands. The Lakota people didn't want to sell the land because it (3) ______________ to them. After lots of fighting, Crazy Horse (4) ______________ and a few years later, Chief Sitting Bull (5) ______________ to the US military.

c) The Suttons talk about the positive things about a small town. Fill the table with two examples each.

Mr Sutton	Greg	Mrs Sutton
• *beautiful nature*	• *rodeo*	• *no traffic jams*

d) ● What do Greg and Mr Sutton say about the Lakota in South Dakota? Complete the notes.

Greg: South Dakota has the (1) *fourth* largest Native American population. Around (2) ______________ Lakota people live in South Dakota. There are five (3) ______________ for the Lakota. (4) ______________ half of them speak the Lakota language.

Mr Sutton: Life on the reservation is (5) ______________. Farming is not easy because the land is (6) ______________. The Lakota make their own laws, but there are social (7) ______________.
The Lakota welcome tourists and they teach them about the Native American lifestyle, culture and (8) ______________ and tell the tourists about the traditions, celebrations and (9) ______________.
In cultural centres, tourists can see fine Native American art and jewellery.

e) After listening, think back over what you heard. Who wants to do what? Write the name.

______________ enjoys a quiet and peaceful holiday.

______________ is very interested in activities.

______________ is interested in culture.

15 WORDS An endless journey (Adjectives with *-ful* and *-less*) ➜ SB (p. 82)

You are taking part in a creative writing competition. The goal is to write the best story you can using the material below.

a) ○ Add the right ending -ful or -less to words in the box on the left to make adjectives. Then match a suitable adjective to nouns in the box on the right. Write in your exercise book.

care · cloud · colour · *end* · event · help · home · hope · sleep · success · use

book · driver · *journey* · mistake · night · man · painting · plan · shop assistant · situation · sky · week

1 *an endless journey*

b) Write a short story of about 200 words. Use at least six of your phrases from a). Write in your exercise book.

*We've just had **an eventful week**. From Monday to Thursday we were all really busy. Then on Friday my dad decided that we should visit my grandmother ...*

16 An email to Mum (Adverbs: word order) ➜ SB (p. 82)

● Matilda writes an email to her mother. Show the correct place of the adverbs by using • and write them on the line above.

Hi Mum, *just*	
I•wanted to send you a quick email to tell you how my first days in Mobridge	just
have been. I'm tired, so this mail won't be long. On the first day it was crazy	a bit, fairly, too
meeting all these new people – who were all – and trying to remember	friendly, hard, very
everybody's name. I'm forgetting people's names, I forgot the name of my host mum, or mom. The first evening my family took me to a festival called *I Hate*	even, still
Winter in the Scherr-Howe Arena. It's used for sports and I thought swimming, because my host sister told me to put my swimming costume on under my	maybe, normally, too
clothes. When we got to the arena, I was surprised when I saw there wasn't a	completely, especially
swimming pool. But as we went inside, it became clear: , it was warm! And	inside, perfectly, so
everywhere was decorated so that it looked like Hawaii. Without the sand, and the Pacific Ocean. But there were stalls selling tropical drinks and music.	exactly
I took part in a dancing competition! It was a complicated dance from Hawaii.	even, quite
I tried to follow the dance steps as as I could. I enjoyed it, but I finished.	a lot, carefully, last
We got to bed late that night, but I could sleep because I was excited. That's all for now, Mum. I hope everything is good with you. xx Matilda	hardly, still, very

17 Drew has a serious argument with his dad (Adjectives after verbs of perception) ➜ SB (p. 83)

a) Copy the table into your exercise book. Write down the words from the box. Add the missing word, either an adjective or an adverb.

angry · bad · carefully · deliciously · good · happily · hard · loudly · serious · strong · real · rightly

Adjective	Adverb
angry	

b) Complete the conversation between Drew and his parents with adjectives and adverbs from a).

Dad: Hi son. Hey, you don't look (1) ______________. What's the matter?

Drew: Well, Dad, I've been thinking (2) ______________ about our trip to Rapid City.

Dad: Me too, son, me too. I can just taste that memorial ice cream they sell at Mount Rushmore. You know it's a special recipe that Thomas Jefferson himself made way back in 1780. It tastes (3) ______________.

Drew: Ice cream in February, Dad? That doesn't sound very (4) ______________ to me. Anyway, Dad, Mount Rushmore is the problem.

Dad: Mount Rushmore a problem? How, son?

Drew: Well, Mount Rushmore is built on land that is sacred to the Lakota. I wouldn't feel (5) ______________ visiting a monument that is (6) ______________ offensive to the Native Americans.

Dad: A monument that celebrates the greatest presidents our country has ever had!

Mom: Hey, who's shouting so (7) ______________ in here? Ben, why do you look so (8) ______________? What has Drew done?

Drew: I haven't done anything, Mom. I just told Dad that I don't want to see Mount Rushmore.

Dad: Drew thinks I don't know my history very (9) ______________. But, Drew, if you look (10) ______________ at the books in my study, you'll see I've read a lot about US history and Native American history too.

Drew: OK, Dad. But it's not just that. I've a friend in school. She's Lakota and she feels (11) ______________ about the Black Hills …

Mom: And it doesn't seem (12) ______________ to visit Mount Rushmore? You know your dad really wants to go there again – it's (13) ______________ important to him.

Drew: Yeah, I know that, Mom. But couldn't I stay in Rapid City while you go to Rushmore? I don't want to make you feel (14) ______________ about going.

Dad: No, Drew. I have (15) ______________ feelings too. We either go as a family together to Rapid City and Rushmore, or you can go to your uncle's while we're away.

c) What do you think? Do you understand Drew's change of mind or do you think that Drew's dad is right? Give reasons.

18 It was extremely offensive (Adverbs of degree) ➜ *SB (p. 83)*

Kaya's and Drew's family feel different about Mount Rushmore.
Copy the sentences into your exercise book and use adverbs from the box to emphasize the statements.
If you think that more than one adverb fits, write two or three.

almost · completely · especially · extremely · fairly · hardly · just · nearly · really · very

1 Like most Lakota people, Kaya's family find the giant faces of the four presidents offensive.
2 In the past, stealing Lakota land and killing the people was heartless of the white man.
3 Kaya told Drew that she couldn't go to the Black Hills because they were sacred to the Lakota people.
4 Drew was disappointed that Kaya wouldn't go with him and his family.
5 When Drew told his parents that he wouldn't go to Mount Rushmore, they were surprised.
6 Drew's brother Austin was looking forward to seeing Drew.
7 Kaya felt sorry when she heard that Drew had been grounded.
8 It was surprising that Drew felt glum at his uncle's house.

19 I completely agree (Collocations with adverbs of degree) ➜ *SB (p. 83)*

a) ○ Using collocations makes your talk more interesting. Match the words to make collocations. Make a list in your exercise book.

clearly · especially · exactly · firmly · hardly · strongly · thoroughly · totally

agree · believe · check · clear · interested in · like · show · surprising

b) Jonas, a German exchange student at MPHS, asks Drew to check his text on the topic: "Should children be allowed to use guns?". Drew highlighted some mistakes in red and now corrects them. Rewrite the correct text in your exercise book. Use the collocations in a) to help you.

In some countries, young people are not allowed to drink alcohol until they are eighteen. It is **not a hard surprise** then that they are **interested** in trying **especially** alcohol once they turn eighteen. Without any experience of drinking, young people can often drink too much and have bad results. In Germany, young people can drink beer and wine from sixteen years of age. Parents can show their children how to drink in a responsible way. I believe it is the same with guns. To me it is **total clear** that when children can learn with their parents how to use guns from an early age, they will be more responsible with guns when they are older.
I **believe strict** that there should be official gun education and training for young people. I also **agree strong** that anyone who wants to buy guns should be **checked** for any negative things in their personal background **thoroughly**, but having official gun training could also be a part of these checks – **like exactly** with cars and driving.

c) Choose one of the topics below and prepare to give your opinion on it in a short talk. Note down some points and include at least five of the collocations from a) and b). Practise your talk. When you are ready, record yourself giving the talk.

1 Learning how to drive should be part of school.
2 Students do not need to learn how to write, they should learn how to type instead.
3 Noone should use social media before the age of 18.

20 STUDY SKILLS Using slides in a talk ➔ SB (p. 84)

Pascal, a student in your class, has chosen to prepare a presentation on the topic of 'Why museums in Europe should give back important cultural exhibits[1] to their home countries' to give to your class.

a) Match the parts of the sentences.

1 In a presentation you should prepare	you got them from. ☐
2 Slides should contain	in a different colour. ☐
3 Your audience should	no more than six lines of text. ☐
4 You can put some keywords	your presentation more interesting and clear. ☐
5 Pictures can help make	as few slides as possible. ☐
6 Remember to write where	your grammar and spelling in your slides. ☐
7 You should always check	listen to you, not read. ☐

b) Pascal shows you three slides which he has prepared for his presentation and would like your feedback. Look at the Skills File on pp. 131–132 in your student's book and write an email to Pascal giving your feedback. Remember to say what you think he has done well and what you think he can do better.

1

WHY EUROPEAN MUSEUMS SHOULD GIVE THEIR EXHIBITS BACK TO THE COUNTRIES WHERE THEY FOUND WERE.

presentation from Pascal Altenbrunn

2

BEFORE THE FIRST WORLD WAR, AFRICA WAS CONTROLLED BY EUROPEAN COUNTRIES.

- Explorers and archelogists travelled all over the continent, searching for important historical and cultural things.
- They found many mummies, jewellery, statues, etc.
- They brought them back to show people in Europe.
- One example is the statue of the head of Nefertiti[2], an Egyptian queen.
- Today, we can see Nefertiti in the Neues Museum in Berlin

3

Why I think we should give these things back

- They don't belong to us. Explorers 'stole' them.
- If we keep them, we are saying to African countries that we can take care of them better because we are better.
- But the world is different now:

1 We know that everybody is equal → Europeans = Africans = Asians
2 There are no more empires and colonies
3 European empires were wrong to take these things from their countries.

c) Prepare the three slides on a computer and follow the tips you gave Pascal.

[1] exhibit [ɪɡˈzɪbɪt] *Ausstellungsstück* [2] Nefertiti [nɛfərˈtiːti] *Nofretete*

21 Did you remember to do your homework? (Verb + gerund or *to*-infinitive) ➜ SB (p. 88)

a) Match the sentences with the pictures.

1 Matilda tried ice-skating and enjoyed it.

2 Matilda tried to ice-skate and hurt herself.

b) In the afternoon people are talking about various topics. Complete the texts with the verbs in the correct form.

TIP: Look at the Grammar File on p. 148 in your student's book and find out more about the difference in meaning when using *forget*, *remember* and *try* with infinitive and gerund. The meaning of *stop* also changes when used with infinitive or gerund:
stop to do sth. = anhalten, um etwas zu tun
stop doing sth. = aufhören, etwas zu tun

1 **Kaya:** Did you remember ____________ photos during the finals?

Drew: Sure I did. We can look at them on my cell phone.

Kaya: Ha ha. Look at that selfie you took. It looks like the horse is eating your ear.

Drew: Man, that looks funny. I don't remember ____________ that photo.

2 On their way to the school library, Drew stopped ____________ his mother that he'd be home late. While they were working on their Boston Tea Party presentations, Kaya and Drew stopped ____________ because Kaya was angry about what the English had done to her people. talk, text

3 **Greg:** What are you doing, Dad?

Mr Sutton: I'm trying ____________ this video presentation on the history of the Lakota tribe, but this switch doesn't do anything.

Greg: Have you tried ____________ the screen? Look, it says 'Play' here on the screen.

Mr Sutton: Oh gosh. I'm so bad with technology, thanks Greg. press, start

4 **Cody:** That was so funny. I'm glad you didn't hurt yourself, but I'll never forget ____________ the look on your face when you fell off Streamer.

Randall: You can laugh. You've fallen off a lot of times yourself. Hey! What about the barn? I hope you didn't forget ____________ the doors again.

Cody: Of course, I didn't. But maybe I should check again. lock, see

c) Write your own sentences in your exercise book.

1 Something you remember doing and something you should remember to do.
2 Something you stopped doing and something you stopped to do.
3 Something you tried doing and something you tried to do.
4 Something you'll never forget doing and something you forgot to do.

22 The Boston Tea Party (Verb + gerund or *to*-infinitive) ➜ *SB (p. 88)*

A classmate has written about the Boston Tea Party. She has made some mistakes with infinitive and gerund verb forms. Tick (✓) the sentences that are correct and correct the sentences with mistakes in your exercise book.

1 In 1773, the British Empire needed money and the East India company needed selling the tea it had in London. ◯

2 The British Parliament wanted making people in the American colonies pay higher taxes on tea from everywhere except the East India company. ◯

3 But the people in the American colonies hated paying these taxes to a Parliament three thousand miles across the ocean. ◯

4 So, in December 1773, when three boats full of tea arrived in Boston Harbour, the people of Boston said they didn't want to buy the tea and it had to stay on the ships. ◯

5 Then, a group of men, who called themselves 'Sons of Liberty', decided taking action. ◯

6 The group pretended being Native Americans, went on to the ships and started opening the boxes of tea. ◯

7 The men loved drinking tea, but they didn't drink this tea – they threw it into the sea. ◯

8 This action was called the Boston Tea Party, and soon people in other colonies stopped to drink tea from England and decided not buying anything from Britain. ◯

9 The British reacted by sending soldiers, but this made the situation worse. ◯

10 The colonies didn't want following British laws any longer – they wanted being free and they were prepared fighting for it. ◯

23 BACKGROUND FILE The Iroquois Confederacy ➜ *SB (p. 89)*

a) Each speaker is one of the five nations of the Haudenosaunee describing their position in a symbolic longhouse. Write in the name of the nation. Give the lines in your student's book that back your answer.

1 ______________________ : The sun shines first on us when we wake in the morning. When I open my eyes I can see its light under the door. We guard the door to protect our brother and sister tribes.

2 ______________________ : The sun lights my way when I lie down in my bed and before I close the door, I see it slide behind the hills. Some of us stay awake through the night to stand guard.

3 ______________________ : I am one of the 'Little Brothers', but not small really. Our brothers, the Seneca, are on our left and the Onondaga on the right.

4 ______________________ : I am the other 'Little Brother'. We wake up early because our neighbours, the Mohawks, greet the sun when they open the door.

5 ______________________ : While our brothers, the Mohawks and Seneca, stand watch over the doors, we also stand watch. We take care of the fire which warms everyone in our longhouse and keeps peace alive.

b) ● The Haudenosaunee learned to live and work together in peace after a time of war. Can you think of other people/countries that have done the same? Give an example and write some reasons.

c) The Haudenosaunee created their confederation in about 1450. In what ways do you think their society and political system was similar or different to a typical country in Europe at that time? Think about: towns, relations with other countries, system of ruling. Write a short paragraph in your exercise book.

24 The end of the world → SB (p. 90)

One of your classmates writes about a Native American legend. Read the text. Then decide whether the underlined words are correct English or not. Write the correct words on the lines on the right.

The Lakota people have a legend about a woman which is real old and lives in a cave somewhere between the Black Hills and the Badlands. She has been in the cave for thousands of years. She is not alone – a huge black dog lies near her and watch her extremely close. She sits next to a fire while she makes a colourful blanket. The blanket is telling the story of life and, as life goes on, the blanket gets longer. There is a pot of Wojapi soup, made by the ansestors of the Lakota, that hangs above the fire. Sometimes the old woman stops to work on the blanket and stands up for checking the soup. She is weak, so she is very slowly at moving. The moment she turns her back, the dog also gets up. He walks over to the blanket and pulls it apart. Then he is lying down again next to the fire. The old woman checks that the soup still smells well and taste delicious, and then she slowly goes back to her blanket. She doesn't see what the dog has done. She continues just her work. For thousands of years now, the same thing have happened. It is surprising hardly that the woman's work is never finished. But she doesn't seem to mind to work on the same part of the blanket again and again. The Lakota say that if the old woman ever completes her blanket, then the story of the life – and the world – would end.

25 Giving a short talk → SB (p. 90) • Wordbank 3

a) For parents' evening you need to prepare a four-minute talk. Choose one of the following topics.

- Choose your own. Think back over what you have learnt in this unit. Choose a topic in the unit that you find interesting.
- The differences between going to high school in the US and *Gymnasium* in your area
- The consequences of the Seven Years' War for the Native American people
- The idea of 'Manifest Destiny' in the 19th century

b) Do research on the topic you have chosen and prepare your talk. You should also prepare slides to go with your talk. Look at p. 84 and the Skills File on p. 132 in the student's book for help.

1 PRONUNCIATION Word stress

29 Say these words aloud and underline the stressed syllable. You can record your voice. Which word has a different stress? Listen and check. Then listen again and repeat the words with the correct stress.

boundary ceremony conflict gallop include patriotism prairie qualify rodeo sculpture

2 About Cody (Gerunds, verb + gerund or *to*-infinitive)

Complete the text about Kaya's cousin Cody with gerunds or the infinitive in the correct form. Use the verbs from the box. Add more words if necessary.

be • bite • catch • clean • do • drive • enjoy • feel • finish • get • go • grin • *live* • make • miss • prevent • ride • stand • tube • wait

Cody thinks that the best thing about (1) *living* on the rez is that he can go riding every evening. He must remember (2) ________ his homework first – that's the worst thing about (3) ________ a high school student, because Cody can't stand (4) ________ homework – but it doesn't usually take too long. In fact, he doesn't remember (5) ________ his daily riding practice even once recently. He thinks that (6) ________ when the sun is going down is awesome. Cody also loves (7) ________ tubing with his friends in the summer. At other times of the year he really misses (8) ________ the wind in his hair as the boat pulls him along. Last time he went (9) ________ he had so much fun that he didn't stop (10) ________ all afternoon – not even when Randall, who was driving the boat, suddenly stopped (11) ________ an accident with another boat and Cody fell out of his inner tube. One thing that Cody's not very good at is (12) ________ fish. He's not very keen (13) ________ there in the cold until a fish decides (14) ________, so he doesn't go ice fishing very often. He has really tried (15) ________ it, but he always gets tired (16) ________. Last time his friend Marc had an idea: "Have you tried (17) ________ bigger holes in the ice?" But it didn't work. Cody really enjoys (18) ________. He'll never forget (19) ________ his driver's license. It was the best day of his life. He's allowed to drive his mother's truck now, but he mustn't forget (20) ________ it once a week.

3 Talking to Drew's parents

30 Imagine that you're an exchange student at Mobridge-Pollock High School and you're staying with Drew. His parents ask you about what you like and don't like doing. Answer each question with at least two sentences. Speak in full sentences and use gerunds. You can stop the recording if you like. Here is an example:

Drew's mother: So, what do you really love doing in your free time?

You: *Well, I like climbing. I go to a climbing centre every weekend. But I really love playing the guitar: I do that nearly every day.*

4 A different kind of party

You are preparing a presentation on the Boston Tea Party for your English class.

a) Talk about this image for about two minutes.
   - Describe what you can see in the photo and what is happening.
   - Say who you think the people are.
   - Say how you think they might be feeling and why.

   Make notes, practise, then record yourself.

b) Listen to your recording. What do you think you could improve next time?
   Then listen again to the recording with your partner and tell him/her what you could do better next time.

5 A short talk

You have to give a two-minute talk on young people's free-time activities in Mobridge. Use the information that you have learned in this unit. Compare the Mobridge kids' activities to kids' activities in Bavaria. Make notes in your exercise book or on cards and prepare to give your talk in class. You can practise your talk in front of a mirror or a partner.

Check: Speaking

a) Vergleiche deine Antworten mit den Lösungen auf den Seiten 71 und 72 im Workbook.
b) Schätze deine Antworten mit einem grünen oder roten Gesicht ein.

		☺	☹	
1	Konntest du in Aufgabe 1 die Wörter richtig und ohne Probleme aussprechen und betonen?	○	○	→ 1
2	Hast du in Aufgabe 3 gewusst, wie man über sich redet und dabei *gerunds* korrekt anwendet?	○	○	→ 2
3	Hast du in Aufgabe 4 ein Bild effektiv präsentieren und beschreiben können?	○	○	→ 4
4	Hast du in Aufgabe 5 die wichtigen Informationen strukturieren, ordnen und einen guten Vortrag halten können?	○	○	→ 3, 4, 5

c) Wenn du dich rot eingeschätzt hast, schau dir die rechte Spalte an.
   Die Nummern führen dich zu den passenden Übungen im Skills Training (S. 58–59).
   Dort kannst du gezielt Speaking trainieren.

1 Word stress

31 Say the words and mark the stressed syllables (just the main stress). Then listen, check and say the words again.

1 excellent	4 property	7 sculpture	10 epidemic
2 qualify	5 support	8 establish	11 offensive
3 buffalo	6 college	9 outbreak	12 relationship

TIP: Word stress is important for meaning. It is often different in German. Use a dictionary to check. Remember:
ˈ = main stress
ˌ = secondary stress
success [sək'ses]
reservation [ˌrezə'veɪʃn].

2 MPHS Radio

a) 32 Kaya interviews an exchange student for the school radio at Mobridge-Pollock High School. Listen to the interview. Take notes on what the student answers to Kaya's eight questions. Write in your exercise book.

b) 33 Now you are the exchange student at MPHS. Use your notes from a) to answer Kaya's questions. Answer each of her questions with at least two sentences. Speak in full sentences and use gerunds. You can stop the recording if you like.

Here is an example:

Kaya: So, you're from Bavaria? Cool! What's the best thing about living there? And the worst thing?

You: *For me, the best thing about living in Bavaria is the countryside: we live near a beautiful lake. The worst thing about living there is that it can get really cold in the winter. I don't like getting out of bed in the morning when it's cold!*

3 Collecting information and structuring a talk

Students from Rapid City are guests at your school. You have to give a talk about the differences and similarities between Rapid City and the place where you live (or your nearest city). First, collect ideas/points. You can do research on the internet. Decide on an order. Write notes in the table that you could use.
Now, prepare and practise your talk.

	Rapid City	Where I live
population		
history		
climate		
geography		
language(s) spoken		
industry		
free-time activities for young people		
sports		
tourist attractions		
famous people/things/places		

TIP: A table helps you to **order your points** so that your talk has a **structure**. Your listeners will understand it better. Complete the table with facts about Rapid City and the place where you live/your nearest city.

TIP: Make notes on numbered cards to **keep the structure** of your talk. Useful phrases can also give your talk structure and make it easier for your listeners to understand it:
- My presentation is about …
- First, I'd like to talk about …
- That's the end of my presentation. Do you have any questions?

4 Talking about an image

You are preparing a talk about the foundation of the US government for an international history event for young people.

a) This image shows the signing of the Declaration of Independence.
- Describe the place and the people. Explain what you think is happening.
- How do the people feel? Why?
- What kind of people are they? What does this say about the world in 1776?
- Explain how this image is connected with the foundation of the US government.

Make notes and practise. Consider the tips in the boxes. Then record yourself. You should speak for about three minutes.

TIP: How to present an image
Say what you can see where:
at the top/bottom · in the foreground/background · in the middle · on the left/right
Describe the parts of the painting in order, e. g. from left to right or top to bottom

TIP: Useful language for describing an image
The following prepositions can help you: behind · between · in front of · next to · under · over

Use the present progressive to describe what somebody is doing and the present perfect to describe something that has just happened: "He is holding the declaration. He has just signed it."

b) Listen to your recording. What could you do better next time? Write notes in your exercise book.

5 Improving your presentation skills

You are going to improve the talk that you prepared for exercise 5 on p. 57.

a) Consider the tips from exercise 3 on p. 58. Are there aspects that could help you to explain the differences in free-time activities better? If you think so, follow the tips and improve the structure of your talk.

b) Practise your talk. Consider the tips from the boxes on the right. Then record yourself. You should speak for about two minutes.

c) Listen to your recording. Is your talk better? What could you still improve? Talk to a partner and give each other feedback. Consider the following aspects:

- Was the talk well structured?
- Did you speak clearly, loudly and slowly enough?
- Did you speak freely - not from your cards?
- Was the talk interesting (e.g. did you give examples and use different adjectives)?
- Did you thank your audience for listening and ask if they had any questions?

Remember: tell your partner what you liked and what he/she could improve.

TIP: How to practise a presentation
Practise your talk at home in front of a mirror or a small audience (parents, grandparents, friends, …). Speak loudly, clearly and slowly.
Look at your audience.

TIP: How to give a good presentation
Wait until it is quiet. Look at your audience.
Say what you're going to talk about and explain the structure of your talk.
Don't just read what is on your cards: try to speak freely.
Thank your audience for listening and ask whether they have any questions.

1 WORDS A crossword puzzle ➜ SB (pp. 34–35)

The words in the puzzle below are related to an event in the 17th century.
Write the answers into the puzzle and find the word in the blue boxes.

1 an adjective that is connected to illustrations
2 to kill somebody as a punishment
3 to make a new, useful object
4 a person who plans a crime together with a group
5 a large fire made in a public place
6 to destroy something by using a bomb
7 to like someone or something for being strong, clever or beautiful
8 when people come together to fight against their government
9 a large, round wooden object that holds gunpowder
10 an object that destroys something powerfully
11 an adjective that describes when everything necessary is included
12 an adjective that describes a person whose identity we do not know
13 a conflict between families, that has been going for a long time, where people might be killed

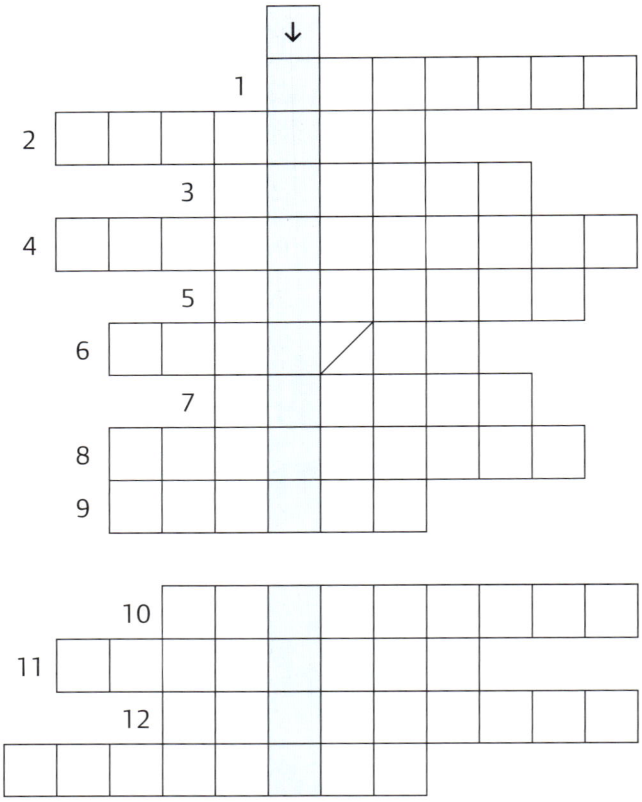

2 The Gunpowder Plot: today and in the past ➜ SB (pp. 34–35)

a) Read the statements. Think about in which paragraph on pp. 34–35 you might find the answer. Check your answer by scanning the paragraph that you have in mind.

	Statement	Text	True	False	Line
1	British children collect newspaper and old clothes before Bonfire Night.	D			
2	The book that made the Guy Fawkes mask famous is set in a very sad and dark London.				
3	Catholicism was invented under the Reformation in the 16th century.				
4	The leader of the Gunpowder Plot was Guy Fawkes.				
5	The film based on the graphic novel was made in 2007.				
6	The Guy Fawkes mask was worn by protesters at the Arab Spring revolts.				
7	King James I's daughter was 16 years old at the time of the Gunpowder Plot.				

b) Are the statements in a) true or false? Tick the correct answer in the table above. Write down the lines where you found the answer in each text.

3 From book to film ➜ SB (pp. 34–35)

**Books are often made into films. Complete the text about film adaptations.
Use verbs from the box in the passive form in the right tense. There are more verbs than you need.**

buy • change • consult with • do (2 x) • employ • find • keep • make (2 x) • move • put across • read • see • show • take out • turn • write (2 x)

If a book is particularly popular, sometimes it (1) ________________ into a film. The book *V for Vendetta*, for example, (2) ________________ about the British government in the 1980s and (3) ________________ into a film in the early 21st century. Some details were different. The book took place in 1997, but of course, this had already passed when the film (4) ________________. So the time of the story (5) ________________ to the year 2032 – "the future". Some people think the film *V for Vendetta* (6) ________________ in order to attract a wider audience. However, the same political message (7) ________________.

Some parts of the original story may need to (8) ________________ for the film. This means that filming can (9) ________________ more quickly and easily. For example, in the eight Harry Potter films, the poltergeist, Peeves, (10) ____ never ________. However, he was a significant[1] character at Hogwarts School in the books.

American author Suzanne Collins' book series *The Hunger Games*[2] (11) ________________ in cinemas in 2012. The author (12) _____ not only ________________ by the producers – the film (13) _____ even ____________ by the author herself, so many details from the original book (14) ________________.

It was a big hit. However, some fans were unhappy and didn't think the books (15) ________________ justice[3] on the screen. But is it really possible to make everyone happy?

4 The fifth of November ➜ SB (pp. 34–35)

You are in London in early November for an international youth project. In a group chat one evening, you see a post from Martim, a boy from Portugal, who is also part of the project.

I've just seen two kids. They were sitting outside a shop with a kind of doll made of old clothes. They asked me to give them money for the doll. They said it was called Guy. Is this normal in London, or were they trying to trick me?!

Reply to Martim's post and tell him in your own words:

- what the children were doing and why
- who Guy Fawkes was and what happened on 4–5 November 1605
- how people celebrate Guy Fawkes Night today
- whether you would like to celebrate Guy Fawkes Night yourself while you're in London and why (not).

Write about 200 words in your exercise book.

[1]significant [sɪɡˈnɪfɪkənt] *bedeutend* [2]The Hunger Games *Die Tribute von Panem* [3]justice [ˈdʒʌstɪs] *Gerechtigkeit*

5 MIXED BAG A library with a difference ➜ SB (pp. 64–65)

Camille from Quebec has written an article for an international youth website about the Haskell Library. Put in the missing words in the correct form. The words in brackets ( ) can help you.

(1) *Have you ever visited* (you – ever – visit) a building where you can be in two countries at the same time? Since the 1900s the Canadian town of Stanstead and the US town of Derby Line, which both (2) __________ (stand) on the US-Canadian border, (3) __________ (serve) by the Haskell Library, where you can do exactly that! The library (4) __________ (build) as a concert hall as well as a place to get books. The building opened in 1904 but it (5) __________ (not – use) as a library until 1905. The Haskell Library (6) __________ (promote) US-Canadian understanding and (7) __________ (= speaking several languages). It is also an interesting place for visitors: inside, a black line (8) __________ (can – see) clearly on the floor, which (9) __________ (let) you stand with one foot in Canadian territory and one in the US! As a resident of Stanstead, I (10) __________ (visit) this library many times since I was a child. In some ways it is just like any other library: it (11) __________ (use) by the local community and the main rule is: "Books (12) __________ (must – bring back) on time or you (13) __________" (fine). Yet, it (14) __________ (can – not – describe) as a typical place in Canada or the US. That is because the rules for moving between the US and Canada (15) __________ (become) tougher since the 9/11 attacks, and passports (16) __________ (must – show) at the 119 official border checks between the two countries. It (17) __________ (be) possible for a Canadian town and a US town to share a post office in the past. But towns (18) __________ (not – allow) to do that for some time now: everyone has to go through a passport check. I am glad that the Haskell Library still lets people from both sides of the border meet and (19) __________ (≈ talk to each other) easily. I think that similar libraries (20) __________ (should – set up) by other border towns around the world.

6 Canadian words and symbols *SB (pp. 64–65)*

a) 34 Listen to Tanya from Alberta. She explains four Canadian words. Match the words to the explanations.

chinook | toque | loonie | tourtière

a one-dollar coin | a meat pie | a warm wind, common in Alberta | a woolly hat

b) 35 Read the questions in b–e. Then listen to the radio show discussion about two of Canada's national symbols and answer the questions. Circle the right letter.

1 How many species of maple tree grow in Canada?

A 10 | B 13 | C 71 | D 150

2 How much of the world's maple syrup is from Canadian export?

A 53 % | B 71 % | C 74 % | D 96 %

3 Which city is home to the Maple Leafs hockey team?

A Quebec City | B Vancouver | C Halifax | D Toronto

c) Which product was most popularly made from beavers during the fur trade? Tick (✓) the correct answer.

1 

2 

3 

4 

d) Cross out the wrong information and correct the sentences.

1 The beaver first became a Canadian symbol in the 16th century. Later, the Hudson Bay Company, which made coats, used the beaver too.

____

2 The beaver was on Canada's first stamp 151 years later in 1851, and it has been on the fifty-cent coin, which was designed by a Canadian artist, since 1937.

____

The first Canadian postage stamp

e) Answer the questions.

1 According to Professor Young, what saved the beavers?

____

2 How does Roula feel when she hears how large the beaver population used to be? _______________

3 Name one Beaver Tail topping that is talked about in the interview. _______________

7 The US political system ➜ SB (pp. 98–99)

First read the tasks a)–d) opposite. Then read the text on the political system of the USA and do the tasks.

Two very important documents

The Declaration of Independence in 1776 helped the US to create the government that it has today. The document stated that everyone is equal and has the right to 'life, liberty and the pursuit of happiness'. Other rights were listed in the constitution and many changes (called 'amendments') were added to the constitution later to give people even more rights (such as not allowing people to be enslaved and letting men and women of all races vote).

A government in three branches[1]

The constitution is the foundation of the US political system, and it splits the federal[2] government into three parts that all have different jobs: the president and the cabinet, Congress, and the Supreme Court and other courts[3].

The main job of the president, helped by the cabinet, is to implement[4] and enforce[5] laws and to help the government to work well. Congress makes the laws. The main job of the courts is to decide on the meaning of the laws and decide whether they are being followed.

The founding fathers created a government with three separate parts so that no single element could become more powerful than the others. They had experienced England's political system and they believed that a country ruled by a king or queen could not always have a good balance of power.

The president

The president is elected for a period of four years and is not allowed to serve for more than two four-year periods. The president has two official homes – the White House in Washington, D.C. and Camp David in Maryland. Every president since John Adams in 1800 has lived at the White House. The president's cabinet is made up of a team of people who give him/her advice on different subjects.

· The White House ·

Congress

Congress is made up of two branches: the House of Representatives and the Senate. They are both made up of elected members. The Senate has two members from each state, who are elected for six years. The House of Representatives has 435 members: the number from each state depends on the size of the population that is being represented, and they are elected for two years. Congress is also in Washington, D.C., in the Capitol Building.

· The Capitol Building ·

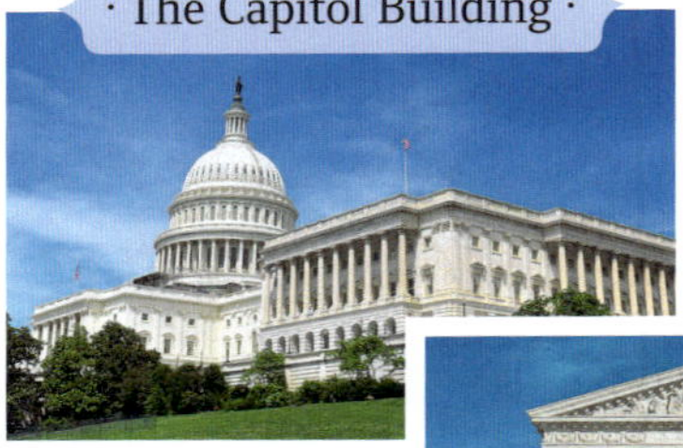

· The Supreme Court Building ·

The Supreme Court

The Supreme Court of the United States is the highest court in the country. It has nine members and they may serve for life if they wish to. They are not elected by the people. Its building is also in Washington, D.C.

Voting and being elected

In 1776, just a few years before the US government was formed, the only people who were allowed to vote in elections were white men who were 21 or older and owned land. Today anybody who is a US citizen and 18 or older can vote, since the rules have been changed over the centuries. However, you have to be 30 or over to be elected to the Senate and 25 or over to be elected to the House of Representatives. To be elected president, a person must be at least 35 years old and a 'natural-born' US citizen.

The main political parties

The two main political parties in the US are the Republican Party and the Democratic Party. They are both powerful and are the only two parties that really have a chance at federal level. For this reason, the US is often called a 'two-party system'. Around a quarter of Americans are members of one of the big parties. This is often so that they may vote in the 'primaries' (the first phase in an American election).

[1]branch [brɑːntʃ] *Zweig* [2]federal ['fedərəl] *bundesstaatlich* [3]court [kɔːt] *Gericht* [4]implement ['ɪmplɪment] *einführen* [5]enforce [ɪn'fɔːs] *durchsetzen*

a) Match the people to the correct descriptions.

1 US president	helps the country's head of state to make decisions on certain topics ☐
2 US citizen over the age of 18	may only work for a certain time and must be over 35 ☐
3 member of the Supreme Court	may vote in primaries ☐
4 member of the Republican Party / Democratic Party	may vote in US elections ☐
5 member of the House of Representatives	may work for six years at a time ☐
6 member of the cabinet	elected for just two years ☐
7 member of the Senate	responsible for the way the US federal government is structured today ☐
8 founding fathers	responsible for checking that laws are followed; may work as long as he/she wants ☐

b) You are helping a friend with a school project. Underline the wrong word/number in each sentence of the text. Then write the correct one on the right.

In 1776, the year that Thomas Jefferson wrote the constitution, you had to be a rich white man in order to vote in an election. Today, all US citizens who are 21 or over may vote, as the rules have been changed in the constitution several times since then. However, if you want to be a member of the House of Representatives or the Senate and present the people of a certain state, you must be older.

When the constitution was introduced, it set the moment for a new kind of political system. This document splits the US Congress into three parts, all with different jobs. The president (elected by the cabinet) is one part, the Senate and the House of Representatives are another and the third is made up of the Supreme Court and other courts.

c) Look at the questions and take notes from the text in your exercise book. Now cover the text on the left and answer each question in 1–2 sentences. Use only your notes.

1 Why did the people who created the US federal government want it to have three different parts?

2 How have the rules about who can vote changed since the 1770s?

3 Why is the US political system described as a 'two-party system'?

4 What is one reason for joining the Republican Party or the Democratic Party, according to the text?

d) The Declaration of Independence states that everyone has the right to 'life, liberty and the pursuit of happiness.' What do you think this idea might mean to different groups of people? Write 50–100 words about each of the following groups in your exercise book. Then share your ideas with a partner. Do you agree with each other?

– the representatives who signed the Declaration of Independence
– the men and women who were enslaved by Thomas Jefferson and George Washington
– the people of the Lakota and Dakota Nations in the second half of the 19th century
– young Americans today

For the representatives who signed the Declaration of Independence, I think that a right to 'life, liberty and the pursuit of happiness' would probably mean the right to live independently from Great Britain and ...

Wordbank 1: Sightseeing

1 Ways to see a city

guided tour
[ˌɡaɪdɪd ˈtʊə]
Stadtführung

double decker
[ˌdʌbl ˈdekə]
Doppeldeckerbus

horsedrawn carriage
[ˌhɔːsdrɔːn ˈkærɪdʒ]
Pferdekutsche

bike
[baɪk]
Fahrrad

viewing platform
[ˈvjuːɪŋ ˌplætfɔːm]
Aussichtsplattform

2 Things to see and do

cathedral
[kəˈθiːdrəl]
Kathedrale

mosque
[mɒsk]
Moschee

synagogue
[ˈsɪnəɡɒɡ]
Synagoge

skyscraper
[ˈskaɪskreɪpə]
Wolkenkratzer

tower
[ˈtaʊə]
Turm

dome
[dəʊm]
Kuppel

park
[pɑːk]
Park

arch
[ɑːtʃ]
(Tor)bogen

column
[ˈkɒləm]
Säule

statue
[ˈstætʃuː]
Statue

fountain
[ˈfaʊntən]
Brunnen

zoo
[zuː]
Zoo

fairground
[ˈfeəɡraʊnd]
Vergnügungspark

flea market
[ˈfliː mɑːkɪt]
Flohmarkt

art gallery
[ˈɑːt ɡæləri]
Kunstgalerie

painting
[ˈpeɪntɪŋ]
Gemälde

In the bedroom

alarm clock [ə'lɑːm]
battery ['bætri]
battery charger ['bætri ˌtʃɑːdʒə]
bookcase ['bʊkkeɪs]
calculator ['kælkjuleɪtə]
calendar ['kælɪndə]
chest of drawers [ˌtʃest‿əv 'drɔːz]
curtain ['kɜːtən]
cushion ['kʊʃn]
drawer [drɔː]
dust [dʌst]
duvet ['duːveɪ]
envelope ['envələʊp]
frame [freɪm]
handle ['hændl]
nail [neɪl]
parcel ['pɑːsl]
pillow ['pɪləʊ]
radiator ['reɪdieɪtə]
sheet [ʃiːt]
suitcase ['suːtkeɪs]
wardrobe ['wɔːdrəʊb]
waste-paper basket [weɪst'peɪpə ˌbɑːskɪt]
window sill ['wɪndəʊ sɪl]

Illustration: Christian Bartz, Berlin

Expressing opinions

Stating what you think

I think/I feel/I believe (that) there are lots of reasons to become a vegetarian.
I'd say (that) your body gets all it needs from things like milk, eggs and vegetables.
I guess/I reckon (that) it would be better for the environment if we gave up meat.
It seems to me that/My impression is that lots of people don't care about animals.
In my opinion/In my view …
If you ask me, …

If you are sure

I'm quite/absolutely sure that you will save money if you stop eating meat.
I have no doubt that …

Giving reasons

We eat too much meat, and **that's the reason why** so many animals are kept in factory farms.
It's a fact that all these factory-farmed animals need food, and **that's why** our rainforests are in danger.
If you look at the number of chickens that get killed every day, **you'll see** why I've decided to become a vegetarian.
Let me explain: …

If you are quoting from a text

The text says in lines … (that …)
If you look at lines …, you'll see …

Agreeing/Disagreeing

\+ **I think so too.**
I think X **is right./I think you are right.**
I agree with X.
That's right/true/correct (but …)

– **I see what you mean but** …
I'm afraid I can't agree with you.
Actually, I see it differently.
I'm sorry but I don't think you can say …
I'm not sure that's a good argument (because …)

Comment adverbs

Fortunately/Luckily, healthy eating has become an issue in many countries.
Unfortunately/Sadly, many people still don't care about what they eat.
Surprisingly/Not surprisingly, lots of vegetarians say they've been feeling fitter since they stopped eating meat.
Ideally, healthy eating should be a school subject.

! Wenn man der Meinung ist, dass etwas nicht der Fall ist, wird im Englischen – anders als im Deutschen – meist das erste Verb *(think, believe, …)* verneint:
German: **Ich finde, das stimmt nicht.**
English: **I don't think that's true.**

absolutely ['æbsəluːtli] *völlig, ganz* I'm afraid … *Leider …* comment adverbs ['kɒment] *Kommentaradverb* (to) disagree [ˌdɪsə'griː] *widersprechen, nicht zustimmen* doubt [daʊt] *Zweifel* fortunately ['fɔːtʃənətli] *glücklicherweise* ideally [aɪ'diəli] *idealerweise* issue ['ɪʃuː] *(Diskussions-)Thema* (to) quote *zitieren* I reckon ['rekən] *ich schätze, ich glaube* sadly *bedauerlicherweise* (to) state *sagen, zum Ausdruck bringen* surprisingly [sə'praɪzɪŋli] *erstaunlicherweise* unfortunately [ʌn'fɔːtʃənətli] *bedauerlicherweise, leider*

Making suggestions – Reacting to suggestions

Suggesting something

Let's go to the cinema/watch a film/…
Why don't we go to the cinema?
Why not go and watch a film?
How about/What about going to the cinema?
I'd like to go to the cinema/watch a film/… What about you?
It would be nice to watch a film. What do you think?
(Do you) fancy a film/watching a film?
I thought we could/might go to the cinema.

Agreeing to suggestions

Good idea.
(That's a) great idea.
(That) sounds great.
Sure, okay.
Oh yes, I'd like that.
That would be nice.

Disagreeing with suggestions …

I don't think that's such a good idea.
I'm not really sure about that.
I'm not so keen on that, really.
I'd love to, but it's late/too expensive/…

… and making alternative suggestions

I'd (much) rather stay at home/go for a pizza/…
Can't we / Why don't we go for a pizza **instead?**
I think it might/would be better to stay at home/go to the youth club/…

Saying what you would prefer

Shall we watch a film or go for a pizza?

I'd prefer the film/the pizza.
I'd prefer to watch a film.
I think I'd rather go for a pizza.

(to) prefer sth. [prɪˈfɜː] *etwas vorziehen; etwas lieber tun* I'd (much) rather … [ˈrɑːðə] *Ich würde (viel) lieber …*

Checkpoint 1

1 Talk like a Londoner

a) 2, 4, 5, 6, 10, 11, 14
b) 2 shall I teach you; 4 glass of water; 5 fish and chips; 6 didn't I say that; 10 you are a natural; 11 you had better watch out; 14 do you want to

2 Murals around London

a) B, C, D
b) There are many famous murals around London. They are also called street art. Each of them tells a different story. Many show dreams, myths or fairy tales. Others are used to carry a message. Some have been covered up with plexiglass to protect them, because sometimes murals are stolen. But more often they are changed/destroyed by the people who own the walls or doors they were painted on because they don't like them.

3 Alyssa in Camden

a) 1 Amy's family set up a foundation in her name.
2 Amy's first job was selling candles at Camden Market.
3 Amy was discovered when she was performing in clubs and pubs around Camden.
4 The artist who created Amy's statue wanted her to look helpless and powerful at the same time.
5 The music programme helps young people start a career in music.
6 The schools' programme helps children learn about the dangers of alcohol and drugs.
7 Amy spent a lot of time living and working in Camden.

b) 1 1 year: Rob's career in music
2 12 weeks: the length of the music programme
3 2 weeks: in that time Rob meets his guide/mentor
4 18–25: age of young musicians
5 3 years: age when children can start a music programme/therapy

Checkpoint 2

1 WORDS Opposites and paraphrases

a) 1 far; 2 unusual; 3 darkness; 4 to love; 5 asleep; 6 together
b) 1 to hit or shoot (a ball)
2 to clear and leave (a place)
3 to follow or not break (a rule)
4 to say funny or silly things
5 to see or hear (something when it happens)
6 to remember something from earlier

2 An exchange visit to Ontario

First steps
You will not be told which school you will be sent to until after Easter, but an information pack should be delivered to your home in the next few weeks. The papers inside the pack must be completed and sent back as soon as possible …

Events and activities
Many special events can be enjoyed during the exchange. A welcome party will be held at City Hall, for example, and exchange students may also be offered the chance to go on an expedition in Algonquin Provincial Park. Camping equipment should not be brought from home, as you will be given everything here in Ontario if necessary.

Rules
The organization's rules for living with host families must not be broken. Guests may not be invited to sleep at your host family's home, but one or two friends from school may be brought there in the evening or on the weekend. You will not be allowed to have parties. Your host family's wishes must be respected at all times.

3 Writing a comment: first steps and …

a) **Berhane**
✓ To find your opinion about the topic, brainstorm some ideas.
✓ Organize your ideas before you write your comment.
✗ Online research takes too much time, so it's better if you don't do it. → Research online. You don't have to read all the search results.
✗ Remember: the information that you find should not change your opinion. → Remember: the information that you find may change your opinion.
✓ Keep your introduction short.

Zaineb
✓ Choose the right search engine settings (e. g. language, country).
✗ Check where information comes from after you have decided to use it. → Check where information comes from before you decide to use it.
✗ There are few useful expressions that you can use to start each paragraph. → There are many useful expressions that you can use to start each paragraph.
✓ Give reasons for your opinion in the main body and use facts to support it.
✗ Don't give your opinion again in the conclusion. → Give your opinion again in the conclusion.
✓ Remember to suggest a solution in the conclusion.

Two more useful tips for internet research, e.g.
- Read the website description carefully before you open a website.
- Skim the first page of a website to check that it has the information that you need.
- Find out where information comes from before you decide to use it.
- Click on the 'About us' page to check if a website is reliable.
- If you want to use a website later, add it to your bookmarks.

4 Writing a comment: structure and …

a) 1, introduction: Young people on school sports teams […]
2, main body: It is often said that gaming is […]
3, main body: Firstly, gamers have to work hard […]
4, main body: Secondly, although many people […]
5, main body: Thirdly, many people are […]
6, main body: For example, in 2018 […]
7, conclusion: It's my hope that in the future […]
8, conclusion: In fact, I would like to see schools […]

b) **individuelle Lösungen; Musterlösung:**
I agree with Kirima's point of view: I believe that esports should be a high-school sport.
It is often said that gaming is not good for teens or not a 'real sport', but like Kirima, I think that it is a sport. Firstly, nobody is naturally good at gaming: you have to practise a lot, just like with football or hockey, for example, so esports are very much like other sports. Secondly, gaming can allow young people who are not able to play traditional sports (or are just not good at PE) to be part of a sports team, which is a great experience. Thirdly, if young people learned about gaming at school, it might help them to learn more about technology, which would be good for their future.
It is my hope that gaming will one day be a sport at schools in my region. We should still do PE, but I think that students should have the chance to learn and practise gaming after school with a coach too.

5 Writing a comment: an exchange year

I do not believe that every high-school student should spend an exchange year abroad before they are 19. In fact, I think that there are many reasons why a young person might not want to go abroad for a year.
There is evidence to support the idea that an exchange year is good for a student's language learning. For example, research by the IES showed that 86 % of people who had studied abroad with this organization believed that the experience helped them to improve their language skills, but in my opinion this does not mean that everyone should study abroad. Firstly, a student may not want to leave their hometown: maybe they have a hobby like sport and they don't want to leave their team, or maybe they just don't want to leave their family. Secondly, it is possible to learn to speak a language very well without living in another country for a year: some young people learn another language at home or in their community, or through shorter trips to other countries. Thirdly, if every high-school student spent a year abroad, it might be difficult to find enough good host families.
It is my hope that young people will be able to decide themselves whether they want to go on an exchange. In my opinion, all high-school students should have the chance to do an exchange year, but it should always be optional.

Checkpoint 3

1 PRONUNCIATION Word stress

boundary; ceremony; conflict; gallop; include; patriotism; prairie; qualify; rodeo; sculpture

2 About Cody

2 to finish; 3 being; 4 doing; 5 missing; 6 riding; 7 going; 8 feeling; 9 tubing; 10 grinning; 11 to prevent; 12 catching; 13 on standing; 14 to bite; 15 to enjoy; 16 of waiting; 17 making; 18 driving; 19 getting; 20 to clean

3 Talking to Drew's parents

individuelle Lösungen; Musterlösung:

Father: Oh, really? And what are you looking forward to doing here in Mobridge?
You: I'm looking forward to seeing a movie at the drive-in. I'm also looking forward to going tubing. It looks awesome!
Mother: Drew hates doing some of the typical local activities like ice fishing. He can't stand the cold. What about you? Are there any activities you don't like doing?
You: I like most local activities, but I don't like dancing, so I wouldn't like to go to a downtown dance.
Father: OK, that's useful to know … We were thinking of taking you to Rapid City on Saturday. We could visit Mount Rushmore, or have a picnic. Would you be keen on doing either of those things?
You: Oh, yes! I'd be keen on visiting Mount Rushmore and seeing the presidents' faces that are carved in the rocks. That would be great.
Mother: OK. There's also a riding center nearby that we sometimes visit with Drew. You could ride a horse there if you like while he's training … And we sometimes stop on the way home to eat an ice cream and see a movie. Are you interested in doing any of those things?
You: Yes, I'm interested in riding a horse at the riding center and seeing a movie later. I'm not really interested in eating an ice cream because I don't like it, but I could eat something else.

4 A different kind of party

Musterlösung:
I am going to talk about this image of the Boston Tea Party in 1773. It shows a very busy harbour. On the left, in the foreground, there is a large ship. It looks like somebody is throwing big boxes into the water. In the middle of the picture – also in the foreground – we can see two small boats with quite a lot of people in them. Most of them are looking at the boat or the boxes. In the background we can see large crowds of people on land. There are so many people that it is impossible to count them. They seem very excited and they are watching what is happening around them. There is a large American flag on the ship and, at the front of the crowd in the middle of the picture, there is a man who is holding a similar flag.
I think the people in the picture are people from Boston who are angry about the taxes that the colonies in North America have to pay to Britain, and that they have no political representation. They have come here to protest. The ones on the ship who are throwing the boxes are local people who are disguised as Native Americans, and they are actually throwing chests of British tea into the sea. I think that they might be feeling angry, or maybe excited because they are finally doing something to show Britain that they don't agree with its laws.
The people in the crowd could be local people who have come to see what is happening. But I think that they are probably protesting too, or maybe they are just curious and want to see what will happen next. The man with the flag is probably a leader of the colonists. I think he might be feeling proud and happy: you can see that in the way that he's standing.
I'm not sure who the people in the two small boats are. Maybe their job is to bring the tea into the harbour on their boats, but they have joined the protest. In this case, I think that they might be feeling angry and excited too. This is a very important moment in American history.
That's the end of my presentation. Thank you for listening. Do you have any questions?

5 A short talk

individuelle Lösungen; Musterlösung:
Hello everyone.
In this presentation I am going to talk about young people's free-time activities in Mobridge and Bavaria.
First I will talk about Mobridge and what young people like doing there. Then I will compare these activities with activities that young people do in Bavaria.
Mobridge is a really small town but there are lots of fun and exciting free-time activities for teens. I'm going to talk about indoor activities first.
Some kids in Mobridge spend time on social media, listen to music and draw or paint. Some of the kids in the book talk about going out for pizza after school too. There is a movie theater in Mobridge that is popular with young people, but another way to watch movies is to go to the drive-in. It is cheaper than the movie theater, but you have to have a car, of course. I think the drive-in must be quite unusual: one boy in the book says that it's one of the last ones in South Dakota. Two indoor events that Mobridge kids can go to in the winter are the downtown dances and the "I Hate Winter" celebration. The dances take place in a tent on Main Street. The "I Hate Winter" celebration takes place in the Scherr-Howe Arena. The kids arrive in coats but then they strip down to their bathing suits because it's hot inside.
There are a lot of outdoor activities in Mobridge. Riding seems to be very popular, and some kids compete in the high school rodeo. Other popular activities are swimming and tubing, which can be done in the Missouri River, and fishing – even in the winter when the water is frozen. Then it's called ice fishing. Some kids like hunting turkey, pheasant or deer, but they have to do a course first. Finally, another popular outdoor activity is driving: some kids love driving around the town and hanging out in their cars.
Now let's compare these activities with what young people in Bavaria do. My town is quite small, like Mobridge, and some of our indoor activities are quite similar. For example, many kids that I know spend time on social media. I also know some teens who like painting and drawing. But there are differences too: gaming is also very popular with my friends, but the Mobridge teens don't talk about that. We have a pizza restaurant here, but I don't usually go there with my friends. We go to the cinema sometimes. I'd like to experience the drive-in, but we don't have one here – or our own cars! I think the downtown dances in the tent are similar to the festival that we have here in my town in the summer, with music, rides and traditional food. We don't have anything like the "I Hate Winter" celebration, but I wish we did! It sounds awesome.
Many of the outdoor activities that are popular in Mobridge are possible here in Bavaria too. My friends and I often go swimming in the lake when the weather is nice, and I also go riding. One big difference is that we don't have rodeos here. I'm not sure whether I would like to compete in a rodeo: for me, riding is just a hobby. Fishing is not so popular with young people here, but there are some teens who do it. I don't know anyone who goes ice fishing in my town. Hunting is another activity that you can do in Bavaria, although we hunt different animals. It's not very popular with the kids at my school. Many of them think it's awful. Two things that we never do where I live are tubing and hanging around in cars. We have no river for tubing, and nobody who is my age has a driver's licence or a car. That's the main difference between Mobridge and my town: kids here need to use bikes, buses or trains, so we have a bit less freedom than the Mobridge kids.
That's the end of my talk. Thank you for listening. Are there any questions?